HOLY LIFE

L. SANTOS

CREATION
HOUSE
A STRANG COMPANY

HOLY LIFE by L. Santos
Published by Creation House
A Strang Company
600 Rinehart Road
Lake Mary, Florida 32746
www.creationhouse.com

Unless otherwise noted, all Scripture quotations are from the New King James Version of the Bible. Copyright © 1979, 1980, 1982 by Thomas Nelson, Inc., publishers. Used by permission.

Scripture quotations marked KJV are from the King James Version of the Bible.

Scripture quotations marked NIV are from the Holy Bible, New International Version of the Bible. Copyright © 1973, 1978, 1984, International Bible Society. Used by permission.

Scripture quotations marked NLT are from the Holy Bible, New Living Translation, copyright © 2007. Used by permission of Tyndale House Publishers, Inc., Wheaton, IL 60189. All rights reserved.

Scripture quotations marked NLT 1996 are taken from the Holy Bible, New Living Translation, copyright © 1996. Used by permission of Tyndale House Publishers, Inc., Wheaton, Illinois 60189. All rights reserved.

Design Director: Bill Johnson
Cover design by Justin Evans

Library of Congress Control Number: 2009924881
International Standard Book Number: 978-1-59979-766-3

First Edition

09 10 11 12 13 — 9 8 7 6 5 4 3 2 1
Printed in the United States of America

For as the rain comes down, and the snow from heaven,
And do not return there,
But water the earth,
And make it bring forth and bud,
That it may give seed to the sower
And bread to the eater,
So shall My word be that goes forth from My mouth;
It shall not return to Me void,
But it shall accomplish what I please,
And it shall prosper in the thing for which I sent it.

—Isaiah 55:10–11

CONTENTS

Chapters and Chapter Topics

INTRODUCTION

Since everything around us is going to be destroyed like this, what holy and godly lives you should live, looking forward to the day of God and hurrying it along.
—2 PETER 3:11–12, NLT

A REOCCURRING THEME THROUGHOUT the whole of the Bible is man's behavior, God's desire for us to live pure and holy lives. In Matthew 3:2, John the Baptist exhorts the people to repent of their sins and turn to God. He then shouts out to the Pharisees and Sadducees, "Prove by the way you live that you have repented of your sins and turned to God" (Matt. 3:8, NLT). Through Matthew 3:7–9, John the Baptist highlights that there needs to be a change of action and attitude within us when we repent of our sins. Just because the Pharisees and Sadducees were descendants of Abraham, it did not mean they automatically qualified to receive eternal life. In the same way, being born into a Christian home, going to church, praying to God (as the Pharisees and Sadducees did), and not breaking the law of the land does not automatically mean we are followers of Christ. Followers of Christ are those who obey God's Word, and through obeying, "truly show how completely they love him. That is how we know we are living in him. Those who say they live in God should live their lives as Jesus did" (1 John 2:5–6, NLT).

I have noticed that many of us who call ourselves Christians have forgotten the principles of living a holy life and live in a very similar way to how the world lives. We lack sufficient fear of God and knowledge of His Word in order to turn from a life of sin back to living a life of holiness. In

Ezekiel 18:24, we are warned that those who turn from righteousness to sin and then die in sin will lose all the rewards and benefits their righteousness would have brought them.

Along the same lines, it has been widely established that to be or become a Christian, no effort is required on our behalf. "Just accept and believe in Jesus and the Cross and you're saved," we often hear. Search the Bible, asking yourself if this is really true. John 17:3 tells us that "this is life eternal, that they might know thee the only true God, and Jesus Christ, whom thou hast sent" (KJV). Being a Christian is about knowing God personally, not a superficial belief about if Jesus existed or not. I personally do not even like the expression we use to convey becoming a Christian—*to accept Jesus*. I think it would be more accurate to say "to make the decision to obey Jesus." It is one thing to believe that Jesus died for the forgiveness of sins, but it is another to give up everything and follow Him.

Many think that whoever believes in Christ cannot go to hell but will go to heaven. However, you can "accept Jesus" all you want, but Romans 6:16 teaches us that if you keep on sinning and do not turn to God wholeheartedly, the consequence is death. (Committing fully to God is actually part of truly believing in His Son). John 8:34–35 also tells us that continuing to live in sin leads to death.

I have therefore decided to compile this book, which searches through the New Testament asking the questions, How is a true believer to act, behave, and think in this world? How should I live my life to prove to God that I have repented of my sins and turned to Him?

At this point it is necessary to mention that this book is not intended to be a recipe for how to please God. It is intended to be a guide full of practical advice designed to help Christians live a life of obedience to God through faith in Jesus Christ within a personal and loving relationship with Him, amidst continual fellowship with the Holy Spirit. If you simply follow the advice and reflect the attributes written in this book, you will not be found righteous before God. It is through a real faith in Jesus Christ that we are made righteous, and the result of this is a deep relationship with God.

Jesus reveals in John 3:5–7 that the only way to enter the kingdom of God is to be born again. By using the phrase *born again*, Jesus is not referring to a second birth through our human mothers; He means being born in the Holy Spirit of God into a new, different life, living by faith and 100 percent for God. This begins with baptism in water and baptism in the Holy Spirit. In Matthew 3:11, we see that to be baptized in water, repentance of sins is required, and John the Baptist refused to immerse the Pharisees and Saddu-cees because of their failure to repent. God wants genuine remorse for our erroneous, dishonest, and sinful ways of living. John prophesied that Jesus would baptize in the Holy Spirit and with fire. The Holy Spirit then dwells in us, where He sanctifies and regenerates us.

The result of this baptism is that our whole outlook on life is completely turned around, and our desires entirely change. It includes renouncing our old life of hatred, unforgiveness, unloving attitudes, evil, and the selfish nature to live a life of love; loving and desiring to serve God, loving all people, even strangers, and forgiving those who offend us when we wouldn't have before. We no longer desire our own, selfish ambitions, but we start to desire the things of God, closeness to Him, the salvation of the people we know and don't know, to be holy, etc. The Holy Spirit inside us teaches us all these things. It is a new life in the Spirit of God, in which we are totally dedicated to God and love Him more than anything or anyone else.

Jesus says, "The Spirit alone gives eternal life. Human effort accomplishes nothing" (John 6:63, NLT). If we try and work hard in our strength to get into heaven, we will fall short because we are all sinners (Rom. 3:23); and God is perfect, so He cannot allow sin in His presence. However, if we enter heaven through Jesus' death on the cross so our sins are forgiven, we will be saved. Then we must try our best to accomplish every command written in the New Testament—this is also called working out our salvation in Philippians 2:12.

The reason this book focuses on commands in the New Testament is because, while holiness is also a dominant theme in the Old Testament, the Old Testament partly defines *holiness* as sacrificing unblemished offerings before God, washings, and purifications. Today, because of Jesus Christ, we no longer need to live in a world of offerings and rituals. Jesus has removed the necessity of daily animal sacrifices and replaced it with His perfect self-sacrifice on the cross of Calvary. He is now our High Priest and representative before God, cleansing our sinful essence and making us new by the presence of the Holy Spirit in our lives.

We must not forget, however, that the Old Testament is still rich in wonderful lessons and personalities, and it reveals much about the glorious nature of God. The Old Testament must never ever be ignored, because it also teaches us so much about our new life in Christ (which is essential to our faith). And of course, the message of the gospel begins in Genesis. We can also even learn much from the different types of offerings acceptable and unacceptable to God, the cleansing and purification rituals, the moral laws, the regimentation the priests had to follow, and the yearly celebrations to be observed, to name but a few. On the whole, they teach us that we should not approach God offhandedly or disrespectfully. We must scrutinize our lives so as not to dishonor or defile God's pure presence within us. We still prepare ourselves before God, but now we do so in a very different way.

In Leviticus, we learn that the Israelites were made "unclean" by eating or touching various animals and carcasses; by skin diseases, including sores, burns, and baldness; by a woman's period; and a man's discharge, amongst many others. These typify man's lack of spiritual wholeness before God. There is nothing we could do to avoid many of these, such as a woman's hemorrhaging after birth and a man's bodily fluids, which are essential to produce offspring and therefore necessary to continue the human race. God is demonstrating that we are spiritually deficient without His intervention—we can do nothing to be made right before Him on our own.

However, we are now made unclean not by outward actions or breaking such rules; rather, in the words of Jesus, "it is what comes out of a man that makes him 'unclean'" (Mark 7:15, NIV). Spiritual holiness is no longer expressed in physical perfection, but through what is invisible to the human eye. Spiritual cleanness now comes in the following form, from 1 John 1:7: "But if we walk in the light as He is in the light, we have fellowship with one another, and the blood of Jesus Christ His Son cleanses us from all sin." So while we are saved as we take the decision to follow Christ, salvation is also a procedure of turning away from old ways and walking in His light.

There is a stark reminder in Mark 9:47 about the urgency to stop sinning: "And if your eye causes you to sin, pluck it out. It is better for you to enter the kingdom of God with one eye, rather than having two eyes, to be cast into hell fire." Jesus cautions us that we can go to hell just because we never stopped sinning, regardless of who we are and what we have done for God and the poor. In 1 John 3:7–10, we are basically told that people who sin and do not love others are children of the devil. I do not want to be called a "child of the devil" by God. Do you?

> Many will say to Me in that day, "Lord, Lord, have we not prophesied in Your name, cast out demons in Your name, and done many wonders in Your name?" And then I will declare to them, "I never knew you; depart from Me, you who practice lawlessness!"
>
> —MATTHEW 7:22–23

Jesus clearly tells us in the above quotation that the way we behave determines whether we will go to heaven or hell. It does not depend on whether we speak in tongues, have an amazing gift of prophesy and healing, go to church, or call ourselves a Christian. It depends on how we act in our everyday life. And according to Matthew 13:41–42, whoever breaks God's law shall be denied their entrance to heaven and will be sent into hellfire: "The Son of man shall send forth his angels, and they shall gather out of his kingdom all things that offend, and them which do iniquity; And shall cast them into a furnace of fire: there shall be wailing and gnashing of teeth" (KJV). This is why it is imperative to know exactly what God requires of us.

We all struggle with sin. We all sometimes find it difficult to give up what we want or are used to doing. Even when we are born into a new life with Jesus, we can still find it very difficult to quit what sin has held us captive to for years. In the same way, Paul revealed weakness in the flesh when he wrote, "For I have the desire to do what is good, but I cannot carry it out" (Rom. 7:18, NIV). As with Paul, often our desire is to stay away from sinning and therefore please God, but even with this thirst, the sin living in us, being as strong as it is, can still manifest itself and do what it craves, not what we want. We sometimes temporarily lose the waging war within and give in to the sin living inside us.

Thank God for His mercy and patience with us as we fight the battle in His strength. And thank Jesus for His blood and body given for us, which means that when we do slip up and practice evil, we can be washed and made clean through Jesus' perfect sacrifice. This, however, does not give us an excuse or license to sin! Instead, it gives us all the more reason to press on and take hold of our death when we died with Christ on the cross, and our new life through His resurrection.

Our dying with Christ involves the crucifying of our old life and therefore our sinful nature and passions, too. Our rebirth means we are free from the power of sin, and consequently we can live in righteousness. This spiritual law gives us the capacity to be more than conquerors over sin and thus to reach out for our victory, giving us strength in the battle against evil.

It is the Holy Spirit who "helps in our weaknesses" (Rom. 8:26, NIV) and "those who live in accordance with the Spirit have their minds set on what the Spirit desires" (Rom. 8:5, NIV). To clarify exactly what this new life in the Spirit comprises, please read on, praying over Psalm 119:27 and asking God to help you to understand the meaning of His commandments.

Chapter 1

A RELATIONSHIP WITH GOD

*The God before whom my grandfather Abraham and my father,
Isaac, walked—the God who has been my shepherd all my life.*

GENESIS 48:15, NLT

G OD IS OUR Holy Father. He is God Almighty, the creator of everything—heaven, Earth, the universe, you and me—but He is also
a personal God and is concerned with even the minute details
of our lives. "But the very hairs of your head are all numbered," declares
Luke 12:7. As He is holy, so He calls us to be holy. The way forward to real
holiness is to spend time with Him and in His Word. The longer we spend
developing a relationship with Him, the more we will become like Him. He
will then impart more grace and knowledge into our lives to equip us to
have a healthy soul, body, and spirit.

The Bible expresses a very personal aspect of knowing God. In Philippians
3:8, Paul writes, "Yet indeed I also count all things loss for the excellence
of the knowledge of Christ Jesus my Lord." This "knowing Christ" does
only not refer to head knowledge, i.e., knowing about Jesus, but also to a
personal enlightenment and intimacy with Him, living closely with Him
and in Him. Through this type of relationship, we are transformed into a
new person, as recorded in 2 Corinthians 5:17, "Therefore, if anyone is in

Christ, he is a new creation; old things have passed away; behold, all things have become new."

This involves leaving our old way of life behind—the old habits, thought patterns, desires, ambitions—and living a new life with Christ Jesus as our focus. Put more explicitly in Galatians 2:20, Paul refers to this as being crucified with Christ, which involves crucifying our old way of life and being born into a new one. Paul even called his old existence a "loss" in Philippians 3:8, compared with his new one.

Such new life is all part of having a rich relationship with God. If we are not born again and do not walk in holiness, it is impossible to have this fellowship with God that our spirit so desperately desires. A major part of having this friendship with the Lord and being saved, is walking in obedience to Him. To enable us to do this, He has given us the Holy Spirit, in whom we should constantly walk.

> I will put My Spirit within you and cause you to walk in My statutes, and you will keep My judgments and do them.
> —EZEKIEL 36:27

Paul explains the meaning of "walking in the Spirit" in Galatians 5:16–17: "I say then: Walk in the Spirit, and you shall not fulfill the lust of the flesh. For the flesh lusts against the Spirit, and the Spirit against the flesh; and these are contrary to one another, so that you do not do the things that you wish." Walking in the Spirit is obeying what God desires, not what we ourselves desire.

Paul makes it clear that living by or walking in the Spirit leads to righteous living, rather than evil behavior. As Christians, we are constantly in a spiritual battlefield. We are continually at war with the world, i.e., we struggle against sin. All sorts of wicked desires and cravings can pounce on us at any time, which then work within us, encouraging us to do not what pleases God but what satisfies our own worldly nature.

God has used King David to illustrate this conflict. When David should have been at war, he stayed in Jerusalem (2 Sam. 11:1). To stress how distracted he was, the Bible says in verse 2 of the same chapter, "Then it happened one evening that David arose from his bed and walked on the roof of the king's house." This sounds slightly strange, because the text portrays a king either sleeping or lounging around on his bed during early evening. (It must have been early because there was enough light to be able to see Bathsheba from a distance.) The first questions that spring to mind are, Did he not have a kingdom to run? and, Were his days filled with lying about in bed? It was at precisely this point that David started lusting after a married woman, and he consequently slept with her. This was not a moment when David was walking by the Spirit; rather, he was seeking after his own evil desires.

Today, by God's grace, we can learn from David's experience. Walking out of the Spirit and being spiritually casual leads to sin springing upon us unawares. Sometimes when we feed the flesh by watching something unhealthy on television, at the movies, in the theatre, on the Internet, or in the street, for example, sinful thoughts can creep into our mind without us even realizing it. This is what happened to David, except the unhealthy use of his eyes was watching Bathsheba bathing. This is why we are exhorted to live life in the Spirit (Rom. 7:6), which keeps us away from distractions and spiritual carelessness.

However, when we are born again, at the same time evil thoughts enter our minds, it is more than likely that our spirit is also fighting, wanting to do what is right. But it can be too easy for us to give into the flesh and let it do what it wants. Jesus explains this theory clearly in Mark 14:38: "Watch and pray, lest you enter into temptation. The spirit indeed is willing, but the flesh is weak." This is why, as Jesus wisely advises, we must always be watchful and constantly keep our thoughts in check. When we are Spirit-filled (and you must be to be saved; see 2 Cor. 1:22), the Holy Spirit inside will warn us whenever our attitudes change and we sin.

Even so, His voice is gentle and soft; "Your ears shall hear a word behind you, saying, 'This is the way, walk in it,' Whenever you turn to the right hand Or whenever you turn to the left" (Isa. 30:21). Notice the word used is *behind* as opposed to *in front of,* which would make heeding His voice easier. But because He speaks behind us, it is easier to crowd out or simply disobey what He says and instead follow the body, pleasing man rather than God.

Jesus tells us that the spirit is happy to do the right thing and obey God, but it is the flesh that will not want this. This is why we must always build up our spirit as much as possible. Whenever possible, we must feed it, that is, through prayer, by reading and studying the Word of God (which cleanses the mind; Eph. 5:26), having fellowship with our brothers and sisters, and generally seeking God in all we do. The Word of God takes away negative thoughts and renews our mind (John 15:3) and is powerful to interrupt the process of depression and other mental illnesses.

We know whether we are walking in the Spirit or not by what dominates our thought life.

> For those who live according to the flesh set their minds on the things of the flesh, but those who live according to the Spirit, the things of the Spirit.
>
> —ROMANS 8:5

When we mostly allow negative and sinful thoughts to dominate our minds and conversations, we are sinning and living in disobedience to God, blocking His revelation to us. As Christians, we must train our brain and imagination to be used for the glory of God. For example, a person may observe a window in a building and visualize pushing someone through it or throwing something against it. However, this person needs self-control to interrupt such thoughts and instead admire the amazing technological and engineering gifts God has given man to create such a window. The eyes are the window of the soul, so we must be wise not only with what we look at but also how we view, touch, taste, smell, and hear things. For those of us who are dominated by a cruel and damaging mentality, it's time to seek God to be transformed by the renewing of the mind (Rom. 12:2).

Having an actual intimate relationship with Him involves talking with Him; adoring Him, sharing our thoughts, and expressing our innermost desires to Him. This involves pouring our souls out to God and weeping in His presence with a thankful heart for all He's done in our lives and because we thirst for Him, His goodness, His loving kindness, His truth, His answers to prayers, and His blessings. There is something very intimate about shedding tears in God's presence. When we sow in tears, we will reap with joy (Ps. 126:5). As we turn to God in times of suffering and difficulties, God's Spirit is our Comforter and is the one who dries our teardrops. When this happens, we are in fact more blessed than the people of the world who have never suffered our same problems (Matt. 5:4).

In Psalm 51, David unreservedly pours himself out to God, confessing his sadness and difficulties. He cries to God and is not afraid of looking like a fool; he knows that is impossible to a loving Father. Grief is a reality in everyone's life and can in fact bring us closer to God. We too should recognize our weaknesses and confess them before God in sincerity. David finishes his prayer by concluding that Jehovah has heard his clamor, showing that God is not a distant God. Sorrow can be overcome as we learn to trust God and His intervention and interest in our lives.

God desires His people to know Him, to have their own personal experience with Him, and to seek new encounters with Him everyday, experiencing salvation, the freedom from sin, life transformation, and His wonderful gifts. Joshua's contemporaries, who were born in the desert, were the generation who knew, saw, and felt God. They were familiar with the Almighty, who guided them with the cloud and pillar of fire and provided for them through manna and from the water gushing out of a rock, and they were present when God spoke to their leader.

Paradoxically, the writer of Judges says a new generation appeared who didn't know God and therefore didn't have the understanding to search for and obey Him. Consequently, Judges is a book of disgrace, embarrassment, and spiritual failure for the Hebrews, whereas Joshua is a book of victories and conquests. Similarly, we undergo spiritual weakness in the church through failure of seeking God for own experiences.

As the human body needs food, so our spirit yearns for God's presence. Spending time with God is the most valuable way to use our moments. God calls us to humble ourselves, turn away from wickedness, and then seek Him with all our heart; thus, we will find Him (2 Chron. 7:14). We need to look to the Lord for His strength and reflect on His character (1 Chron. 16:11–12).

Seeking God's face is more than just saying a prayer. It's being face to face with Him and getting close to Him, not talking in a hurry but exploring Him, and therefore becoming more like Him. The Lord wants closeness with His people. He always had someone He revealed Himself to in the Bible, such as Enoch, Noah, Moses, Elijah, and Daniel. Our Creator called Abraham a "friend of God" (James 2:23) and even communicated to him before destroying Sodom and Gomorrah. Therefore, naturally, as we get to know God, we will reveal our own identity to Him clearly and calmly, and He will see our sincerity.

One practical way of doing this is to study God's Word, not just reading it but actually doing our own study of a passage or biblical topic. This shouldn't be done in a rush or under pressure, but wholeheartedly, attentive to God's voice. His Word sanctifies our mind (John 17:17) and brings us peace and stability (Ps. 119:165). It teaches us how to walk in holiness and truth as we strive to copy Him in all He does (John 5:19). The Lord desires to pass on what He has to us—His grace, love, and peace —and will do so as we get nearer to Him.

If we are His followers, all our decisions must be oriented around Him, searching for either His permission or interdiction in every aspect of our lives. James 4:13–15 encourages believers to add the phrase *God willing* to our future plans. This practical advice can help us to always place God's plans before our own. It also teaches us that God is the leader of our decisions and steps along the road of life, not ourselves. We must not put God in a bottle, seeking to make Him accessible whenever we want; rather, we need to place Him as Master of all our decisions all the time.

King David is a fine example of someone who asked God about plans and actions for the future. He often inquired of God about governmental issues and regarding military arrangements (2 Sam. 5:19) because of his very familiar and functional relationship with God.

Jesus says of people who carry out God's will, "Anyone who does the will of my Father in heaven is my brother and sister and mother!" (Matt. 12:50,

NLT). Remember that we know nothing about the future; we may think we do, but we don't. Only God knows and only God's way is safe, so we should follow it. Jesus goes even further than this, declaring that those who do not do His Father's will (i.e., whoever carries out their own will in life) are not actually saved: "Not everyone who says to me, 'Lord, Lord,' will enter the kingdom of heaven, but only he who does the will of my Father who is in heaven" (Matt. 7:21, NIV).

Part of this closeness required by God is loving Him with all our heart, mind, body, and spirit above everything else. Paul wrote that God is He "by whom we cry out, 'Abba, Father'" (Rom. 8:15). *Abba* means "Father" in Aramaic, and Jesus used the same word when He taught His disciples to pray. A more literal translation into English would be "papa," communicating warm intimacy as well as reverence. God wants us to refer to him as "Papa"—our Father in heaven who is the closest one to us.

One woman showed warm, devoted, and rich fellowship with God in the gospel of Luke: "And behold, a woman in the city who was a sinner, when she knew that Jesus sat at the table in the Pharisee's house, brought an alabaster flask of fragrant oil, and stood at His feet behind Him weeping; and she began to wash His feet with her tears, and wiped them with the hair of her head; and she kissed His feet and anointed them with the fragrant oil" (Luke 7:37–38). This lady had spent a lot of money to purchase the rare perfume she poured over Jesus' feet. She did this because she found mercy and love from someone who accepted her. She probably had never experienced this type of acceptance before because she had only been used and abused by other men as a prostitute. She therefore decided she would spend possibly all she had to anoint Jesus' feet, the least glamorous and dirtiest part of the body, the part of the body that is most often on the floor.

Through this, we learn that when we spend our money to glorify God and pass time in His presence, we please Him. This woman had to go through the effort of gaining access to Simon's home and kneeling on the floor, weeping in front of people who completely despised and disrespected her. This either took much courage and sacrifice, or her complete newly-found devotion to God meant that she did not allow herself to feel belittled by the presence of the "superior" Jews. What is interesting about this lady is that she may have used her tears to clean Jesus' feet. Tears do not come at a monetary value. They are unique and individual to each one of us. They are completely priceless to God. God does not want only our sacrifice, which today most often equates to time and money; He wants our whole heart and immediate obedience to Him.

> Has the LORD as great delight in burnt offerings and sacrifices,
> As in obeying the voice of the LORD? Behold, to obey is better
> than sacrifice, And to heed than the fat of rams.
>
> —1 SAMUEL 15:22

As mentioned at the beginning of this chapter, obedience to God is a key element in our relationship with Him. (See Chapter 6, "Purity.") Jesus goes as far as claiming that whoever does not obey God does not have eternal life in them: "He who believes in the Son has everlasting life; and he who does not believe the Son shall not see life, but the wrath of God abides on him" (John 3:36). In the first part of this verse, the word *believes* in this English translation can be deceptive. In the original manuscript, it means believe and obey. We find in Mark 3:11 that the demons certainly accept Jesus as God's one and only Son: "And the unclean spirits, whenever they saw Him, fell down before Him and cried out, saying, 'You are the Son of God.'" Therefore it is made clear that only knowing that Jesus is God's Son is not enough. We have to surrender to Him, which includes following His commands and leading a holy life.

James explains this more clearly, "Do not merely listen to the word, and so deceive yourselves. Do what it says" (James 1:22, NIV). The word *do* in this verse means that action needs to be taken in order to please God. (See the section entitled "Faith with Works" in Chapter 3.) Again, Jesus clarifies the meaning of the word *believe* in John 6:29 by referring to it as work: "Jesus answered and said to them, 'This is the work of God, that you believe in Him whom He sent.'" We do not receive eternal salvation by attending church meetings, feeling pious, and just agreeing that Jesus died on the cross. We receive it by responding and acting positively to what is written in the Bible. Unfortunately, this aspect of faith has become lost in many Christian circles and needs to be revived before any more people are deceived.

Furthermore, false doctrines often emerge in the church. One is the appearance of a shift from spiritual concerns to only seeking Jesus for what He can do for us, for His physical provisions. The reactions of the crowds that followed Jesus were not much different than what we are sometimes like today. In John 6, after Jesus provided for the people's material needs during the feeding of the five thousand, they became so excited and enthusiastic about Him that they tried to make Him king by force (John 6:15). Such honor and excitement toward Him were superficial, in the same way hype and exhilaration can sometimes be in church nowadays. After Jesus' reprimand the following day, it became evident that the crowd was only after temporary, worldly things of no spiritual importance. Jesus then explained the deeper, spiritual meaning of the miracle; that the bread symbolized Himself and that He could spiritually sustain them better than edible bread and fish. When the crowd realized meeting their physical needs was not His primary concern, "many of his disciples turned back and no longer followed him" (John 6:66, NIV). In the same way, many turn away from Christianity today when they see difficulties arise or when what they hoped for is not fulfilled. They become disillusioned with God because they have not built their house on the rock but on sand. Sometimes it is through no fault of their own; it is because they have not been taught the true essence of the gospel message but rather a man-made one.

GOD AS NUMBER ONE

The LORD is your life.

—DEUTERONOMY 30:20, NIV

We must steadily keep our hearts and spirits on fire for God, with our eyes fully fixed on Him. This includes striving to represent and reflect him wherever we are—in bed, at the dinner table, at school, church, work, home, driving along, in the street, in the supermarket, etc. Living in such a way will cause joy to overflow in our lives as we constantly concentrate on the hope set before us.

The life of a zealous person is characterized by dedication to and incessant searching through the Scriptures, studying God's Word, fervency in prayer, and complete denial of self. Our greatest enemy sometimes is not the devil. It can in fact be our own selves. The devil is not omniscient. Who's with you twenty-four hours a day? You are! The devil sends his demons out, but he cannot dominate everything. We must deny ourselves and our own will every day, maintaining incessant communion with God, reflected by righteous living.

The Holy Scriptures tell us that God must be the most important aspect in the lives of believers. This is typified in the New Testament by the disciples who surrendered everything for Jesus: "Immediately they left the boat and their father, and followed Him" (Matt. 4:22). If there is anything in our lives that comes between God and us, our calling is to either give it up completely or put it to the side and maintain our focus fixed on the God who provides for all our needs. Additionally, Jesus warns: "You cannot become my disciple without giving up everything you own" (Luke 14:33, NLT). It is clear God demands our 100 percent, undivided attention, not to be shared with anyone or anything. Jesus knew that possessions and riches are a tremendous temptation and contender for the number one spot in our hearts because of the immediate but superficial satisfaction they bring. (See Chapter 10, "Riches.")

The Lord even requires us to constantly dwell on Him: "I will bless the LORD at all times; His praise *shall* continually be in my mouth" (Ps. 34:1). If we ever feel ourselves thinking about something or someone else more than God, our alarm bells should be ringing that we need to seek God to get our priorities right. God will not share our love with anything or anyone, which is why we have to be careful when we find ourselves devoted to a certain television program, web site, subject, book, property, person (spouse, child, famous personality, friend, family member), film, music or style of music, country, culture, studies, church, animal, dream, or job. It can be very easy to place any one of the aspects aforementioned (although the list is not exhaustive) above the importance of God in our lives. When we do this, it is idolatry, a deceptive trap for present-day Christians because the idols of today are not as obvious as they were during Bible times, although possibly today's gods appeal more to our senses. They can seduce our sight through beauty and lustfulness, and they feed our flesh, leading to gluttony.

Especially in the Old Testament, God is often depicted as a jealous God: "You shall not bow down to them nor serve them. For I, the LORD your God, am a jealous God" (Exod. 20:5). This is reflected more forcefully as Jesus fulfills the Old Testament laws: "Don't let anyone call you 'Rabbi,' for you have only one teacher... And don't address anyone here on earth as 'Father,' for only God in heaven is your spiritual Father. And don't let anyone call you 'Teacher,' for you have only one teacher, the Messiah" (Matt. 23:8–10, NLT). Jesus is saying that there should be no earthly representation that takes the place of Him in our lives. We must always look to God for our needs, hopes, dreams, desires, etc., and not substitute Him with a religious figure. Some people have gotten into the habit of calling their church leader "father," which goes directly against the above scriptural quote. Others look to Mary as their source of hope and the one to whom they pray, even though she was a normal, mortal human. Jesus wants us to focus on the fact that through His death on the cross, we have been given direct access to God. Our sins have now been forgiven and we can pray directly to God. He is our Father, Teacher, and source for everything.

Anna, a prophetess from the book of Luke, is a sound example of a zealous nature. After her marriage of only seven years ended, she probably felt she had nothing to live for, except her hope in God. The Gospel tells us that she "did not depart from the temple, but served *God* with fastings and prayers night and day" (Luke 2:37). She surrendered her time and whole self to God's glory, not allowing anything to distract her. She also spoke to everyone who wanted to hear about Israel's Redeemer, devoting herself completely to His truth. She was passionate about God and His promise, which was made manifest in how she spent her days and what she spoke.

As well as being zealous for the Lord just like Anna, we should display enthusiasm for the things of God, such as eagerness for righteousness, good works, and heavenly things. Paul demonstrates this clearly in 1 Corinthians 7:29–31 when he inspires the Corinthian church to put aside anything which may distract them from the way of godliness. He writes, "Those who have wives should live as if they had none; those who mourn, as if they did not; those who are happy, as if they were not; those who buy something, as if it were not theirs to keep; those who use the things of the world, as if not engrossed in them" (NIV). Paul urges his readers to shake off all preoccupations and have only one goal in life—pleasing the Lord. Paul is conscious of the frailty of this life as well as man's weaknesses. If we are not careful to be zealous in our faith by stepping away from what could divert the mind from Jesus, we may be tempted to give up the race.

In 1 Corinthians 9:24–27, Paul describes the Christian life using athletic metaphors, such as a race to be run (KJV). He implies that there is to be no slowness or dawdling. Instead, he emits energy and enthusiasm to the readers by his choice of language, encouraging us to be full of motivation and devotion as we run toward our eternal reward, firmly rooted in Christ the Rock.

During the Christian race, since we go through the different circles and processes of life, as humans, we may sometimes find ourselves feeling discouraged. When our soul feels demoralized, it provokes lethargy, neglectfulness, and listlessness in the faith. In the middle of the night, the disciples, tired from lack of sleep and exhausted from fighting strong winds, were rowing frantically. They surely felt disheartened at Jesus' disappearance; therefore, perhaps they were suffering a slight dip in their faith levels at the time. Suddenly they became terrified when they saw a ghost-like figure walking on water. Just before despairing, they heard Jesus' voice, "Take courage! It is I. Don't be afraid" (Mark 6:50, NIV). Jesus' words were exactly the words they needed to cure their dampened spirits. It is likely their fright and fear completely vanished on hearing these encouraging words. Jesus is giving us this same message when we feel down and lacking in zeal. He calls us to remember who He is and the wonders He has done for us. He challenges us to trust Him during such times and believe He is the answer to all our worries and problems.

Always remember that our relationship with God is our most valuable possession in life.

FEARING GOD

> And I say to you, My friends, do not be afraid of those who kill
> the body, and after that have no more that they can do. But I will
> show you whom you should fear: Fear Him who, after He has
> killed, has power to cast into hell; yes, I say to you, fear Him!
>
> —LUKE 12:4–5

A very common belief among Christians is that the fear of the Lord does
not involve being afraid of him; rather, it involves a respect and reverence
for Him and His Word. However, in the context of the verse quoted above,
Jesus starts off by comparing the fear of God to being frightened of people
who want to kill you! If you knew there was someone who wanted to put
you to death and was actively seeking your murder, would you be terrified
of them or would you just respect and revere them? Jesus is telling us that
in the grand scheme of things, it is wrong to tremble before them; rather, we
should fear God—literally be afraid of Him—because He can have us killed
at absolutely any moment. In addition to that, He can send us into eternal
hellfire. Paul advocates being scared of God again in Romans 11:20–21. The
reason? If we fall into unbelief and lose our faith, God will not spare us
from death.

> But they were broken off because of unbelief, and you stand by
> faith. Do not be arrogant, but be afraid. For if God did not spare
> the natural branches, he will not spare you either. (NIV)

If you knew that God could strike you dead in a short space of time
just for taking Him lightly and deciding to accept someone's worship for
yourself instead of correcting them, would you be afraid of Him or just
respect Him? This is exactly what happened to Herod in Acts 12:23. If
we were scared of God in this way, knowing that within any moment He
could strike us dead, as He did Ananias and Sapphira, such an attitude
would lead to complete submission to His Word and deterrence from sin.
The result would be real holiness and a life completely dedicated to Him.
We need to adopt such fear of God in our lives, making us obedient to

everything He says and wholly honest in all we do. Aaron was prohibited from entering God's presence whenever He wanted, on pain of death (Lev. 16:2). We still need to be careful before the Lord and check how we come in to His presence.

The psalmist who wrote Psalm 119:161 trembled with fear at God's Word even in the face of persecution from influential people: "Rulers persecute me without cause, but my heart trembles at your word" (NIV). In his model behavior, notice that in a fearful situation, the focus is not on the serious problem at hand, but on God's Word. If the church also literally trembled with fright as we got to know more of God's Word, we would also hate dishonesty (v. 163), be more prayerful (v. 164), and be more obedient (vv. 167–168). Paul also shows us that the fear of God leads to a holy church when he writes, "Let us cleanse ourselves from all filthiness of the flesh and spirit, perfecting holiness in the fear of God" (2 Cor. 7:1). We must therefore quiver before God's Word. Such a response leads to immediate obedience to it, no questions asked.

Paul reveals that his fear of God is his motivation in 2 Corinthians 5:10–11. In verse 11, he writes, "Knowing, therefore, the terror of the Lord." If we look at what precedes "therefore," it should explain how Paul interprets "the terror of the Lord." In verse 10, we are told, "For we must all appear before the judgment seat of Christ, that each one may receive the things done in the body, according to what he has done, whether good or bad." Through fearing the Lord, Paul looks toward the future and is conscious that all he does will be judged, so he is motivated to give everything he has to evangelize ("persuade men," v. 11) and pour himself out to the church (vv. 12–13). In the body of Christ today, we also need to be looking to the future judgment, so then we will give ourselves more fully to carrying out God's will and be more dedicated to His people, as Paul was.

We need to recognize that what Jesus says isn't always what we want to hear. It doesn't always satisfy us or bring us immediate joy. For example, when the rich young ruler in Luke 18:18–22 approached Jesus to ask what he must do to receive eternal life, Jesus practically rebuked the man because of his greeting. Then, just as the man thought he was going to receive a response such as, "Well then, eternal life is yours," he heard something that saddened him: "You still lack one thing. Sell all that you have and distribute to the poor, and you will have treasure in heaven; and come, follow Me" (v. 22). The young man was certainly not hoping for such a challenging response. How often do we come before the Lord expectantly and are only attentive when the answer is what we want? We need to listen to what God says, rather than only hear what we want to hear. The man wasn't happy with Jesus' reply. We need to be careful that when God talks to us about delicate things, such as our behavior, habits, and priorities, for example, we do not shut Him off. We should also realize that it is possible for the Lord to be angry or unhappy with us. Therefore we ought to be very careful when we tell people, "Jesus is smiling at you," or "God is pleased with you," because only He knows in whom He truly delights.

There are many promises in the Bible for those who fear God. To name but a few, such people will be wise (Prov. 15:33), pure (Ps. 19:9), they will lack nothing (Ps. 34:9), be delivered from evil (Ps. 34:7), and live a blessed life (Deut. 5:29). Through the redemption of our sins on the cross of Calvary, Jesus has enabled us to serve God without fear of eternal destruction and hellfire, in holiness and truth, every day of our lives (Luke 1:74–75).

WORSHIP

> God is Spirit, and those who worship Him must worship in spirit and truth.
>
> —JOHN 4:24

Worshiping God is the act of adoration, strong love, and intense dedication toward Him. It is commanded throughout the Old and New Testaments and is part of our devotion to and relationship with God. It is a natural side effect that takes place within our spirit when we are born again. We worship God through the way we live our lives. Life is full of choices to make, and whenever we choose good over evil or to obey the Spirit's direction rather than our own logic, we are worshiping Him.

In John's Gospel, Jesus is called "truth" (John 14:6). In line with the above quote from John 4:24, we can only truly adore the Father if we come through the Son—through the forgiveness of sins on the cross. The quotation also refers to adoring God according to His Word, which is His truth. The Word of God is attributed to Jesus in John's Gospel. Therefore our ability to glorify God depends directly on our obedience to His Word. Without obedience to His Word, we are not worshipers at all, even if we think we are. This type of worship points to magnifying God with our spirits, an act in which our whole being lifts itself up and surrenders completely to God. Being able to exalt God in spirit and in truth is only possible with rebirth, when the Holy Spirit is present in our lives and gives us the grace to do this.

God rejects superficial adoration, which is not done in spirit and truth. In fact, such "worship" is not worship at all. It is a misuse of the word. David believed that if worship did not cost him anything, it was not authentic. We read this in 2 Samuel 24:24, where David insisted on paying Araunah for his sacrifices to God. This goes for us today as well. When there is sacrifice—such as death to the flesh and worldly desires, for example—that is the type of love God requires.

Sometimes simply singing songs to God in our flesh is referred to as worship in the church today, but the way to express the worship defined above is through how we live our lives. It is reflected in our everyday attitudes, actions, and behavior. It is a life of dedication to God's truth and Word. Sometimes we can be fooled and believe we are worshiping God when in fact we are not. The Israelites fell into this snare in the Book of Hosea. Even though they were seemingly virtuous and religious, acknowledging Him and zealously offering Him their sacrifices, which was a form of worship under the old covenant, God rejected them (Hosea 6:1–3; 8:13). This was because they had disobedient hearts. They were not giving their all to God and were only committing to Him halfheartedly.

PRAYER

Continue earnestly in prayer, being vigilant in it with thanksgiving.

—COLOSSIANS 4:2

Prayer is the name given to spiritual communication with God. It is simply expressing ourselves to God. It can take the form of invocation and contemplating God, as well as intercession and pleading. It is an essential part of our Christian walk. Can you have a very close relationship with someone but not speak or communicate with them often? Impossible! Prayer in the Bible is shown to be a frequent activity. In 1 Thessalonians 5:17, we are encouraged to "pray without ceasing," and in Philippians 4:6, Paul directs us to "be anxious for nothing, but in everything by prayer and supplication, with thanksgiving, let your requests be made known to God." From this we can see that prayer must be a) constant, b) full of thanksgiving, and c) asking God literally about anything and everything, including personal issues and for other people.

Jesus focuses on perseverance as an important component of prayer in two different parables in the Gospel of Luke. One is the parable of the persistent widow in Luke 18:1–8, in which the widow does not stop asking the city judge for justice until she gets the desired results. This suggests that those who persist in their faithful requests to God will be quickly granted justice, because if an unjust judge awards an impartial outcome to someone who never gives up, how much more will God, who sent His Son to die for us?

The other parable is in Luke 11:5–10, in which a man is bold in asking his neighbor for food for another traveling friend. Again, Jesus teaches us that whoever has the audacity to keep on asking for something expectantly will certainly receive it. We need to follow this pattern when we pray, although we must be wary of asking for things that are outside God's will.

Our attitude in prayer needs to be, "If it is Your will, I request so and so. If it is not Your will, change my heart about this matter and guide me through Your Spirit." We need to always ask God to make His desires ours. We also should be aware of the temptation to focus our prayers on ourselves rather than on the Lord. Thoughts of Him and lifting Him up in prayer should be the center, not ourselves or what He can do for us, however spiritual our requests may be.

Now, post–old-covenant times, we possess an extra weapon. We are called to ask for things in the name of Jesus (John 14:13; 16:23). This gives us power in the spiritual world, although it is not intended to be abused and used as an excuse to ask for things beyond God's will. James 4:3 tells us, "When you ask, you do not receive, because you ask with wrong motives, that you may spend what you get on your pleasures" (NIV). It is through the new covenant and reflecting Him in character, mind and purpose that we can use this powerful tool. We therefore must be submitted to the Holy Spirit to pray through faith.

Jesus also shows us in Matthew 7:7 that we must not expect to receive anything if we have not actually asked God for it. Often we are taught in church to declare that the things we want are ours and believe they are, and then we will receive them. It seems we may have lost the focus on God. It is He who gives us gifts, so it is to Him that we need to direct our requests instead of just declaring it to the air. We need to believe God for it, not believe in the power of our own words. If we don't ask, we will not receive. See Joshua 15:18–19, where Caleb's daughter Acsah asked, perhaps cheekily, for springs of water in addition to her land. Her request was granted.

Another aspect of prayer life that Jesus instructs on is the need for prayer to be both personal and public. In Matthew 26:36 Jesus tells His disciples to "sit ye here, while I go and pray yonder" (KJV). He is demonstrating that prayer is sometimes a very individual time, which can only be done in private. At other times, it may be right to pray with friends or in public. Jesus described the power of agreement in prayer when He said, "Again I say to you that if two of you agree on earth concerning anything that they ask, it will be done for them by My Father in heaven" (Matt. 18:19). This gives us the opportunity to pray for others, laying hands on them (Acts 6:6). But we must never ignore the need to have a secret, special time with just ourselves and God. This is what builds up intimacy with God and knowledge of Him and His will. Jesus, whom we should imitate, "often withdrew into the wilderness and prayed" (Luke 5:16). In the same way, frequent solitary sessions with God are essential if we are to continue on the Christian walk without slipping away.

Jesus' fundamental teachings on prayer are found in Matthew 6:9–13. His basic structure is the following: the adoration and glorification of God; the presentation of requests, namely for God to provide for all our needs spiritually and materially; and the declaration of God's greatness and focusing on God's eternal nature.

King Jehoshaphat's prayer was well structured and neatly organized, too (2 Chron. 20:6–12). First he praised God for His power and might. He then brought up God's faithfulness to Abraham and God's commitment to the Israelites for help in times of calamity. He then presented the problem and declared that God was the only answer to the situation.

All Christians are given the ministry of intercession and prayer. Intercession is praying on behalf of other people or for certain objectives. It is making requests to God for Him to intervene in lives or circumstances. It is putting ourselves in the gap, where God will operate to bring about His purposes. For example, Moses placed himself as mediator between the people of Israel and God when He pleaded with Him to not destroy them in Exodus 32:11–13. Because of his intercession, the Lord relented (v. 14). Samuel was also a great intercessor, and he knew that it would have been a sin if he had stopped praying for God's people (1 Sam. 12:23).

God calls us to do the same for His children. In Luke 10:2, Jesus commissions us to pray that the Father would send out missionaries to harvest people into His kingdom. We should also be interceding for everyone to come to salvation, including for people in positions of power and with political influence (1 Tim. 2:1–2).

Prayer and intercession are times to listen intently to what the Holy Spirit is saying and then to follow His guidance. Sometimes He may put urgent prayers on our hearts that need to be brought before Him without delay. Or God's Spirit can suddenly bring to mind someone we may have forgotten so that we can act as a go-between.

On other occasions, God may not actually want us to pray for something or someone, which is why it is so important to be attentive to and interlinked with His Spirit. For example, He ordered Jeremiah not to intercede for the people (Jer. 7:16) because the Lord had already ordained their destruction. Jesus also clarified in His prayer, "I do not pray for the world but for those whom You have given Me, for they are Yours" (John 17:9). Jesus knew the Father's heart so well that He knew what to and what not to pray for. The goal of every Christian must also be to pray in line with His will.

Intercession takes all sorts of forms and subject matters. Jesus interceded in His own name (John 17:11) for protection, holiness, and the unity of His followers, while Esther fasted for God to intervene in the forthcoming destruction of the Jews. Elijah prayed sincerely for a drought; thus, no rain fell for three and a half years. He then prayed for rain, and God answered him (1 Kings 18:42). Paul mediated for the Ephesians, requesting the Spirit of wisdom and revelation to be present in their lives so they could grow in God; know the hope Jesus gives; and be strengthened in faith, love, and understanding (Eph. 1:17–18; 3:16–18).

The right attitude in prayer is that of submission to God in order to pray according to His will and not our own. This requires humility and giving ourselves over to the Holy Spirit as we put aside our own desires and requests to follow His. Continual meditation on God is needed to achieve this attitude (1 Thess. 1:2–3), and thanksgiving and praise is often accompanied by intercession (1 Tim. 2:1). (See section entitled "A Sacrifice of Praise" in Chapter 7.)

Chapter 2

LOVE

Though I speak with the tongues of men and of angels, but have not love,
I have become sounding brass or a clanging cymbal. And though I have
the gift of prophecy, and understand all mysteries and all knowledge, and
though I have all faith, so that I could remove mountains, but have not
love, I am nothing. And though I bestow all my goods to feed the poor, and
though I give my body to be burned, but have not love, it profits me nothing.

1 Corinthians 13:1–3

LOVE IS THE essence of God's inner nature. As the central part of His character, through His immense love, He yearned to express Himself and create beings to love. So, He created the world as a manifestation of this supreme emotion, and humans for Him to demonstrate such love to. He has uttered this love and wishes to have a relationship with us by sending His Son Jesus Christ to the earth and sacrificing Him on the cross. Through the greatest demonstration of love in mankind's history, we are now called to love God above all and to love one another (Mark 12:30–31).

Paul describes love as eternal, the only characteristic and emotion we can contain that lasts forever. He insists that whoever does not have love is worth nothing. Actions, words, gifts, sacrifices, talents, knowledge, and wisdom, if produced without love, are all completely meaningless. If love is the inspiration for the aforementioned, only then will they be acceptable to God. Love is altruistic and is faithful even when it is unrequited and the receiver is difficult and ungrateful. We are only able to love in the right way by the Holy Spirit placing it in our hearts (Rom. 5:5).

Love is so crucial that Jesus declares that loving God fully and loving your neighbor as yourself is the summary of the whole of God's law (Matt. 22:37–40). Love is the main ingredient of faith. Without love, true faith is nonexistent (Gal. 5:6). Peter exhorts this fervent love because "love will cover a multitude of sins" (1 Pet. 4:8) and an unloving attitude in us means we will not get into heaven (1 John 3:14–15).

God is the fountain of our love toward all people (1 Thess. 3:12). Those who have love from God do not fear anything because it is impossible for love and fear to coexist (1 John 4:18). Real love within us, which comes from God, is a confirmation of our salvation, so there is nothing to be scared of in life—not death, nor any man, nor the devil, nor any court case or unjust law. Those who know the Lord personally and therefore have experienced His love understand that all that happens occurs with His permission, so there is no reason to worry or be afraid. God's love is a safety net on which we can wait and trust in fully, while enduring every circumstance and situation that confront us in life (1 John 4:16). This works only if we live constantly connected to God's love, as it fills and guides us in every step.

Proof of God's love within is the presence of the Holy Spirit in us, pouring love into our hearts (Rom. 5:5). The Lord's affection toward His chosen people goes beyond what humans can comprehend because it is so strong and yet so tender. Its faithfulness is greater than we can imagine. Christ was sent to Israel because of God's fidelity to Abraham. God kept His promise to him, even though He had no obligation to and could have gotten away with not fulfilling it because Abraham was just a mortal, powerless man. But God was still faithful to the man, though he had died many centuries before Christ.

As we grow in knowledge of His love, we are molded by it, causing a change in our actions and personality. This continual transformation in our lives manifests itself in good works and fruitfulness (2 Pet. 1:7–8). It is often preached in churches to already saved Christians that God loves you just the way you are. This discourages the transformation His love naturally brings and breaks the cycle of change it produces. It is a lie of Satan that encourages Christians to live life how they want to rather than in obedience to God's requirements.

Deuteronomy 7:12 tells us that with those who obey God and live according to His high standard of holiness, God will keep His covenant of love. However, in 8:20, we are warned that whoever does not pay attention to His Word and lives in disobedience to His way of living will be destroyed. So we can see that before receiving salvation, God loved us even though we were bad. If, once we have knowledge of His saving love and are following Jesus, we then decide to live in noncompliance with His truth, God will no longer allow us to experience His love nor pour His blessings on us.

When we do not have love inside us, the Bible tells us we cannot know God (1 John 4:7–8), we are murderers (1 John 3:15), and that we are not saved (1 John 2:9–11). Love is what distinguishes us from all other people on Earth, and it is the key to living a life that glorifies and pleases God, for "love covereth all sins" (Prov. 10:12, KJV) by promoting forgiveness and often by avoiding the offense in the first place.

The amount of love God requires from His people is not modest or easily reached. He requires our love to be so strong that everything in our lives is surrendered to Him. We have to place him first and foremost before everything; before our family members and friends, before pleasures, desires and attitudes; before all the decisions we make, we must always be overflowing in love for God. Jesus says, "He who loves father or mother more than Me is not worthy of Me. And he who loves son or daughter more than Me is not worthy of Me" (Matt. 10:37).

God also expects us to give up everything for him: "If any man will come after me, let him deny himself, and take up his cross, and follow me. For whosoever will save his life shall lose it: and whosoever will lose his life for my sake shall find it" (Matt. 16:24–25, KJV). For most, this is a very hard thing to do. It is natural to have our own ambitions regarding the future and maybe a career, our own ideas regarding where we want to live, what we want to do, and who we want to do it with. However, we must let that go, handing over to God all our dreams, desires, even what we think our calling is. We must say to Him, "Your will, not mine," live by faith, and trust in the Lord as we love Him more than our own lives. Just remember that Jesus gave up everything for us, as He was sentenced to a horrifying death for no crime as a sinless man.

It is very easy to say that we love God and experience real love for Him, but if it is not the right amount of love, it is not sufficient. The way to test our hearts and find out if we really love God with all our hearts, souls, and minds is through our everyday actions and attitudes. When we find ourselves constantly checking whether what we are doing is pleasing or not to the Holy Spirit and we do nothing without His approval, we know we must be on the right path. When we find ourselves slipping into sins often, then it is most likely that we are not loving God will all our heart. Jesus illustrates that when we have the amount of love God requires from us, we will automatically obey His teaching.

> Jesus answered and said to him, "If anyone loves Me, he will keep My word; and My Father will love him, and We will come to him and make Our home with him. He who does not love Me does not keep My words."
>
> —JOHN 14:23–24

Our whole life is a sacrifice of obedience to Him when we love Him as we should. Loving God in the right way leads to hatred of sin and evil, automatically qualifying us for God's protection from the wicked (Ps. 97:10). The only way to love God like this is through the Holy Spirit working in our hearts (Col. 1:8).

One illustration of biblical love for God is in Psalm 73:25–26:

> Whom have I in heaven but You? And there is none upon earth that I desire besides You. My flesh and my heart fail; But God is the strength of my heart and my portion forever.

The psalmist demonstrates utter dependence on and necessity for God. He is passionate about the Lord and knows that He is the only reason for hope and the only One who can sustain him. Everything else in the world is nothing compared to what the Almighty means to the author of this psalm. He recognizes that the Lord is the only eternal element in life and that nothing else is worth chasing after. He literally clings to him (Deut. 10:20, NLT).

Jesus cautions us that losing the first love we experienced at the outset of our new life in Christ is a decoy we should be careful of. In Revelation 2:4–5, Jesus accuses the church in Ephesus, "Nevertheless I have this against you, that you have left your first love. Remember therefore from where you have fallen; repent and do the first works, or else I will come to you quickly and remove your lampstand from its place—unless you repent." Jesus does not tolerate those who fall from their original, innocent, childlike love they received when they became a Christian. He is accusing the Ephesian church of being lackadaisical and growing cold. Jesus forewarned us about this regarding the importance of keeping oil in our lamps (Matt. 25:1–13). Letting our love run dry means we are not persevering in the Christian walk, and we will find ourselves turning back to the old worldly ways of living. (See Chapter 12, "Lukewarmness.") Jesus will not permit such people to enter into eternal life (Matt. 25:10–12), only those who put God first and foremost before everything. Placing God in the number one position in our hearts is also emphasized in the Ten Commandments, where this is the first commandment (Exod. 20:1–7; Matt. 22:37).

After loving God before anything else, we must also be kind and show our love to everyone, paying particular attention to other brothers and sisters in Christ (Gal. 6:10). Our calling is to love fellow Christians sincerely, without falsity and with real concern for their well-being, with devotion and dedication, honoring them before ourselves (Rom. 12:9–10), always wanting the best for them without ulterior motives. All members of the body should, through genuine love, try their hardest to avoid offense and criticism and instead encourage and build up the brothers and sisters in the faith in every way, so the members can live in peace and harmony (Rom. 14:19). Together with faith, love is to be worn as a breastplate (1 Thess. 5:8) because it is used in battle to protect us from suffering harm from the attacks of our enemies.

We are called to love each other as Jesus has loved us (John 13:34). The depth of love God calls us to have for our brothers and sisters in Christ is the same as the love Jesus has for us—love that is capable of even giving up one's own life for others (1 John 3:16). Such love is proof that eternal life is in us (1 John 3:14). Loving other Christians with brotherly love (Heb. 13:1) includes not seeking our own selfish pleasures and satisfaction, which could harm anyone, but instead pursuing the edification of the body of believers (Rom. 15:1–2). This means that in everything we do we are careful not to damage the welfare of fellow believers.

This level of love involves an attitude of longsuffering, in which we feel for our brother in the faith, suffering with him in his sufferings, weeping with him, rejoicing with him, not copying his emotions but identifying with what is happening in his life (Rom. 12:15), and demonstrating real sympathy (1 Pet. 3:8).

It also means we should humbly accept everyone in the body no matter what his social standing is, making sure we deny our own feelings of vanity and self-worth in order to put others first (Rom. 12:16). This includes showing consideration in everything, even in spiritual matters when others are weaker in the faith than us (Rom. 14:21). We should be patient with such people, supporting them earnestly and not just tolerating them but accepting them (Rom. 15:7).

A person full of love from the Holy Spirit is naturally gentle and patient; he or she never reminds anyone of their faults or brings up humiliating mistakes, problems, or stories. They do not correct or rebuke publicly but are considerate and sensitive to the feelings of others (Col. 3:12–14). Christians need to be a people who let go of negative occurrences in the past, forgive, forget, and keep moving forward to the future.

The love that God pours into our hearts for our Christian brothers and sisters encourages peace and avoids arguments (Prov. 10:12). This love forgets and never again mentions offenses (Prov. 17:9). It demonstrates gentleness, humility, and patience, supporting one another lovingly and trying its hardest to live in peaceful unity (Eph. 4:2). Whenever disagreements arise—which are bound to happen, as God did not make everyone the same—we must swallow our pride and give in to the will of others. Even if we think the other people should be humble themselves and give in to our will, we need to remember that they are accountable for their behavior, as we are, and in humility think of them as better than ourselves (Philippians 2:3).

An important attribute to remember in loving our brothers is instant forgiveness, no questions asked, because Jesus has forgiven us and never even demanded an explication from us regarding our past sins. Paul writes that we should forgive "one another, even as God in Christ forgave you" (Eph. 4:32). God did not put a condition on His forgiveness, nor did it depend on our previous actions or prior righteousness. Neither should our forgiveness for our neighbors.

Paul reprimands an unloving approach toward one another regarding filing lawsuits. He challenges attitudes and asks, "Why not just accept the injustice and leave it at that? Why not let yourselves be cheated?" (1 Cor. 6:7, NLT). Paul reminds us that the "turn the other cheek" doctrine must be used in daily situations in order to live a life that pleases God.

Love in the church brings about unity, because it gives everyone the same will to work and serve and unites them with the same goals, objectives, motivation, heart, love, and spirit, so that everyone is "mutually encouraged by each other's faith" (Rom. 1:12, NIV). Such unity brings about corporal growth in the wisdom and knowledge of God (Col. 2:2–3), building peace and edifying the family of believers (Rom. 14:19). This is a description of a perfect church in a perfect world, a church in which everyone carries each other's burdens (Gal. 6:2). However, because we are not perfect yet and are still being perfected, this is not always the reality. Instead, we should make it our goal, with each person doing their part, to live in harmonious love and unity with other believers.

In order to do this, we need to endeavor to have "equal concern for each other" (1 Cor. 12:25, NIV). Love does not honor one part of the body of Christ over another part; so anyone, no matter what their gifting is, who thinks they should be honored above other brothers in Christ is wrong and is not acting in love. The body of Christ is interdependent, regardless of every individual's function. Paul tells us that the parts of the body that seem to be less important or weaker are actually absolutely necessary (1 Cor. 12:22). Through unity, God has given all the parts equal honor (1 Cor. 12:24), in order that some won't demand or receive more respect than others. Through this equality we can rejoice and suffer together (1 Cor. 12:26). Moses experienced this type of unified love for the Israelites when he was prepared to suffer eternally for them (Exod. 32:32), as did Paul (Rom. 9:3).

Such bona fide devotion to our brothers and sisters in the faith is displayed and worked out through actions and emotions. Love encircles all our social obligations, so we will instinctively prove our dedication to one another by good works (Gal. 6:10). For example:

- Sometimes our dedication is displayed through generosity (2 Cor. 8:7–8) when gifts (monetary, physical, or sacrificial) are bestowed voluntarily and freely rather than under pressure or due to guilt, with pure motives, for the benefit of the receivers and the glory of God. This includes meeting the material needs of others. If we do not do this, then the love of God is not in us (1 John 3:17–18). Paul mentioned that not providing for our blood family is a denial of faith (1 Tim. 5:8).
- It is also demonstrated through serving one another (Gal. 5:13.) (See the section entitled "Servant Heart" in Chapter 13.)
- Dedication is evidenced as we teach one another in love, gently correcting sins because of earnest concern about the salvation and spiritual health of one another (Gal. 6:1). (See Chapter 13, "Spiritual Maturity.")
- Helping all by encouraging those who need it, lifting up everyone in prayer, warning those in sin, and meeting the spiritual needs for all the saints shows our dedication as well. Love motivates hard work for the kingdom (1 Thess. 1:3), where we must pursue love (1 Tim. 6:11) and encourage each other in it (Heb. 10:24).

Jesus tells us that our love for our neighbor will prove to the world we are His disciples (John 13:34–35). It can be easy enough to love other Christians, our family and friends, and those who love us, but this commandment Jesus left us includes loving those we don't even know. That includes the stranger on the street; the person who left a mess in the restaurant, taxi, or public place just before we arrived; our next-door neighbors, even when they play loud music we dislike until the early hours of the morning; the person who stole our son's or daughter's virginity; the person at work who always makes life difficult for us; those who spread malicious rumors about us and the ones we love.

The command "love your neighbor as yourself" (Matt. 19:19) should provoke us to think how we would want to be treated if we were our own employee, cleaner, boss, waiter, husband or wife, son or daughter, mother or father, secretary, customer—and then treat them the same way. Compassion to everyone through love is what God has shown to the world, and therefore we should, in turn, display sympathy to others.

Jesus illustrates love for one's neighbor in the parable of the good Samaritan in Luke 10:30–37. The Samaritans were infamous enemies of the Jews, and both cultures taught their communities to hate and despise the other. This gives the story an extra thrust, as Jesus distinguishes insignificant religious beliefs from pure love. He shows that racism and prejudice are unacceptable and that love crosses the boundaries race and generalizations bring. Whenever we are tempted to believe or agree with what one group of society teaches about another (for example, about "women drivers" or judgments about the customs of a particular race), we must remember this parable, hold our tongue, and ask Jesus to change our heart.

What is also significant in the parable is the great sacrifice the Samaritan made for the victim. The Samaritan had to walk on foot because he allowed the victim to occupy his donkey, and he put no limit on what was to be spent on the man's health. Neither discomfort nor financial obligation got in the way of serving a stranger, even an enemy from his society's point of view. Jesus calls us to have exactly the same attitude and to act in exactly the same way as the Samaritan. Love is expressed when we look after the homeless, orphans and others without families, or a steady and adequate income (James 1:27).

God reveals His goodness to the whole of mankind with no differentiation between Christians and non-Christians (Matt. 5:45). In the same way, we should act like true children of God by loving the unkind and ungrateful and loving those who persecute and hate us. After all, God is good and faithful to them, and we should be too. Our aim is perfection because God is perfect (Matt. 5:48).

Christians will always find they have enemies on Earth wherever they are, whether as a corporate group or as individuals. Jesus warns us that "if they have called the master of the house Beelzebub, how much more shall they call them of his household?" (Matt. 10:25, KJV). As aliens in this world, the world cannot accept us. Persecution will come to Christians, so we must be as wise as snakes and guiltless as doves (Matt. 10:16) in our attitudes and actions.

Jesus states:

> But I say to you, love your enemies, bless those who curse you, do good to those who hate you, and pray for those who spitefully use you and persecute you, that you may be sons of your Father in heaven.
>
> —MATTHEW 5:44–45

This can be very difficult to do sometimes, especially when someone repeatedly hurts us emotionally or physically, on purpose or not. Anyone in the world would automatically hate such a person and wish bad things on them. However, as children of the Most High, we have to be different than them.

> But if you love those who love you, what credit is that to you? For even sinners love those who love them.
>
> —LUKE 6:32

Praying for our enemies is a sign of true love toward them and a sign the battle of good against evil has been won. Paul recommends praying for God's blessing on their lives: "Bless those who persecute you; bless and do not curse" (Rom. 12:14). Stephen exemplified such love. As he was being stoned, he cried out, "Lord, do not charge them with this sin" (Acts 7:60). He counted the loss of his life as nothing and showed utmost concern for God's judgment of his murderers. Unto death, Stephen showed undying love for his enemies.

We must be careful to not even gloat or feel satisfied when our enemy falls down (Prov. 24:17), but rather we should mourn because of their downfall and genuinely desire their good. It is a powerful weapon to pay evil or insult with love and blessing (1 Pet. 3:9).

Other ways to stand out from unbelievers is to show genuine love in attitude and action to those who treat us badly or unfairly. This includes lending to them without expecting to get anything back (Luke 6:35), which provides us with a great eternal reward; providing for their material needs, such as giving them food and drink (Rom. 12:20); helping them out with anything they have difficulty with; and always treating them with the utmost respect.

When someone purposely puts us down, attacking us where it hurts the most, we must stay calm and not lose our patience. We should wait for his attack and temper to calm down, trust God that the wave will pass over, and then love will triumph. A rash reply is nearly always regretted. During confrontations, it is usually wiser to stay quiet than to speak. Remember that love does not judge, condemn, humiliate, nor put down; so we ought to give life and not death.

Our freedom in Christ is a reason to prove our love to those who hate and want to harm us. The fact that we are no longer slaves of sin means that because of the love deposited in our hearts by God, we are given freedom to love everyone, regardless of their status and how much they dislike or hate us. When we show real *agape* love, it is evidence of genuine faith (John 13:35) and sends out a message of God's love to the world.

Chapter 3

FAITH

For assuredly, I say to you, if you have faith as a mustard seed,
you will say to this mountain, "Move from here to there," and
it will move; and nothing will be impossible for you.

MATTHEW 17:20

AITH IS UNQUESTIONING credence and confidence in God. Hebrews defines *faith* as "being sure of what we hope for and certain of what we do not see" (Heb. 11:1, NIV). It is what salvation rests upon because faith alone saves. Love does not save, although it can lead us to faith and therefore salvation. In order to possess eternal life, a genuine act of faith is necessary to believe that Jesus is God and that He died for the forgiveness of sins. This act of faith is obedience to His teachings and receiving Him into our lives to totally transform us. In the words of Habakkuk, "the righteous will live by their faith" (Hab. 2:4, NLT 1996), so our faith then becomes the center of our lives and is paramount in the Christian walk.

Jesus' teaching on faith focuses on the physical or spiritual result that takes place due to the work of faith in a person's heart. Jesus seems to concentrate on the outcome of faith, such as a miraculous answer to prayer, the healing of an infirmity, or the salvation of someone's soul. Jesus teaches us not to doubt God's ability or desire to fulfill our requests as we ask for things in prayer but to believe He has done them (Matt. 21:21–22). Often such belief demands a genuine step of faith to be convinced that He will actually do it. Therefore, faith can involve human action, such as in Luke 8:44, when the woman who suffered from bleeding for twelve years reached out and touched Jesus' garment to receive her healing.

Jesus stresses the importance of faith by telling many infirm people throughout the Gospels that it was their faith that healed or saved them.

> And Jesus said unto him, Receive thy sight: thy faith hath saved thee.
>
> —LUKE 18:42, KJV

In the case of the paralyzed man, it was his friends' faith that healed him: "When Jesus saw their faith, He said to the paralytic, 'Son, be of good cheer; your sins are forgiven you'" (Matt. 9:2). In the same way, we can use our gift of faith for the good and well-being of other people and ourselves as we present our requests to God, trusting and believing He will carry them out to completion. We must always be sure to give the glory to God rather than giving ourselves the credit for having faith.

Regarding sicknesses and diseases, sometimes God miraculously heals us to display His glory (John 9:3). Other times, our infirmities may be reflections of sin or spiritual problems in our lives, so praying for supernatural healing doesn't always have an effect. In such cases, we need to ask God to show us where the problems lie and reflect on our lives, seeking the Lord for the renunciation of all sins and growing in the faith to get closer to Him. Isaiah 53:5 conveys that Jesus heals us completely, so if we find He, in fact, has not healed all our medical conditions, it may be a sign we need to give more of ourselves over to Him and obey Him in every area of life.

Faith can be erroneously viewed as a power or way for people to get what they want from God. Many people seek faith for prosperity, healing, and other material blessings. Some churches teach the power of the mind to combat pain and misfortune, and the power of the tongue to confess perfect health. (The latter actually leads to dishonesty.) They say Christians should declare success and prosperity in their lives and even try to control things using brainpower and the influence of the imagination. They encourage the practice of calling things into existence using visualizations, a positive mental attitude, positive confession, and commanding God's blessings into being—all in the name of "faith."

But this mind manipulation has absolutely no biblical basis, and in fact these ideas originate in occultism. The concept stems from the thought that we are mini-gods who have the power to reach for our maximum potential because we are divine beings. This belief is partly taken from Jesus' quotation of Psalm 82:6, "Ye are gods" (KJV). But this excerpt refers to two realities. The first is that God made us in His image, so we have some physical similarities with Him. The second points to Genesis 3:22, when the Lord stated that man became like Him in knowing the difference between good and evil after Adam sinned. So because of Adam's rebellion, we became gods through disobedience to the Lord, and now each one of us judges what we think is good and evil, rather than living by the Creator's standard of what good and evil are. Even the context of Psalm 82:6 is man's perversion of justice. Naturally, the Bible says there is only one God, the Lord Almighty (Exod. 20:3).

Of course, preaching that faith will provide everyone with whatever they desire makes a church grow. This includes the teaching that we can prophesy over one another on demand and by faith. But prophecy is a gift of the Spirit in which God speaks through someone, so it is divinely initiated; it does not happen by man. The mass always likes to hear that they can get what they want just by believing and ordering it to happen, but Jesus tells us to ask for things in His name, not to speak them into existence. We need to be cautious of incorporating heretical practices into our teaching on faith and using the name of Jesus to please our carnal desires.

This sort of doctrine causes churches to produce hyped-up congregations greedy for earthly things rather than true disciples of Jesus who pray, fast, are sanctified, and grow in faith. The actual goal of faith is salvation (1 Pet. 1:9). Its most important function is for us to get into heaven, then its second priority is for earthly things. True faith makes people love Jesus so much that they would let go of everything for Him. We need to make sure church does not become a social place that just causes the congregation to feel good and happy about themselves because "whatever they desire is theirs;" rather, it should be a place where people have their hearts 100 percent turned toward Christ because they love and fear Him so much.

Paul's writings on faith center around trusting in who Jesus is, His teachings, and what He accomplished on the cross, as well as being confident that eternal salvation results from a life of commitment and obedience to God. Paul also stresses that we do not receive eternal life by following a list of rules. It is by faith through the grace of God that empowers us to live a righteous life.

> This Good News tells us how God makes us right in his sight. This is accomplished from start to finish by faith. As the Scriptures say, "It is through faith that a righteous person has life."
> —ROMANS 1:17, NLT

Notice that Paul did not claim that it is through faith that anyone has life. He stated that righteous people who have faith will receive life. Unfortunately, godliness is not often taught together with faith nowadays. We seem to have drilled that anyone can have faith, forgetting what this verse says about the type of people who possess saving faith. Faith without upright living is not faith at all. But when we obey God and live according to His standards, righteousness and faith go together. There is no separation between the two. Through faith we are made righteous, and therefore we will live out a righteous life. Paul also describes the byproduct of faith as "a right relationship with God" in Romans 4:13 (NLT).

If you die the day you decide to follow and obey Jesus, then that is all you need for salvation. But if you do not die on the same day, your faith and therefore your relationship with God needs to be strengthened and must grow. Every day that we live on the earth, we run the risk of losing our salvation if we do not allow our faith to develop.

Growing in the faith is partly a human action. In 2 Peter 1:5–7, Peter urges us to make a great effort to add goodness, knowledge, self-control, perseverance, godliness, brotherly kindness, and love to our faith. Faith needs to be active as we seek God to mature in His truth and attributes while we try our hardest to imitate Him more and more. As we grow spiritually, our faith becomes enriched.

Peter points out that difficulties lead to growth in the faith. He urges believers to understand the value of their faith during trials, realizing that it is greater than their suffering (1 Pet. 1:6–7). It is in distress that our faith will be proved genuine. Pure gold is soft and unpractical; therefore, it is prepared and refined with fire in order for it to be useful. In the same way, faith without refinement can be soft and useless. Thus, the purification that suffering brings and the addition of goodness, knowledge, and self-control make it hardier. This is exactly what happened to Peter's faith. Near the beginning of his Christian life, he thought his faith would never allow him to deny Jesus (Matt. 26:33), but he was soon proved wrong and disowned Jesus not once but three times. By the end of his life, his faith had grown so much that he reached a faith level at which he was willing to be crucified for Jesus Christ.

Each step we take upwards in the faith, we will see things we couldn't see before. God takes us on a journey of sanctity, righteousness, dependence on Him, joy, and strength. In order to progress in the faith, we need to pass through problems and trials. Many of these surface as we carry out our good works. Just remember that faith is necessary to please God (Heb. 11:6) and that remaining faithful to Him is the only way to prove our authenticity as Christians.

Of course, it is clear that Paul was convinced that faith alone saves the soul, as explained in Galatians 3:11 and Ephesians 2:8–9, so we do not receive eternal life through our own efforts and our own works. However, he does go on to say in Ephesians 2:10 that when we are justified by faith, we will naturally go on to carry out good works, according to God's will: "For we are God's workmanship, created in Christ Jesus to do good works, which God prepared in advance for us to do" (NIV). Good works are a natural result of growing in faith and love for God and our neighbor. James explains it another way in James 2:14 by declaring that faith without good works is useless, dead, and does not save.

Faith with Works

I preached first to those in Damascus, then in Jerusalem, and also to the Gentiles, that all must repent of their sins and turn to God—and prove they have changed by the good things they do.

—Acts 26:20, nlt

Paul's preaching tactic is quite different from what we hear nowadays. He taught that whoever wants to become a follower of Christ must change his or her life around for the good and prove it by their good works! Have you heard of that as an evangelism technique lately? Normally we preach the gospel as easy, attractive, and full of blessings, rather than a change of lifestyle with good deeds as a necessity and proof. We need to mix the good news of the gospel with a bit of the fear of the Lord and firm biblical teaching.

According to Matthew 25:31–46, during the Final Judgment, God will separate the "sheep" from the "goats." The sheep, on His right-hand side, enter eternal life; the goats, on His left, pass into eternal punishment. What will determine who the sheep are and who the goats are? Our deeds and actions—whether we help the poor and needy or whether we decide to ignore them. Don't think, "I have prayed the sinner's prayer and accepted Jesus in my life, so I'm saved." God's Word does not say that. God wants our righteous deeds to shine before us. He wants us to see to the needs of those who lack. His will is for us to feed the hungry, give a drink to the thirsty, clothe the naked, care for the sick, and visit prisoners.

There is no shadow of doubt that God's heart goes out to the poor in all ages. He characterizes Himself as a defender of the poor (Exod. 22:22–24; Ps. 140:12), and the Mosaic law contains some rules that were specifically drawn up to help and support poor people, such as the command to leave gleanings for them (Deut. 24:19–22). Again and again in the New Testament, the poor are remembered, and stress is put on serving them: "All they asked was that we should continue to remember the poor, the very thing I was eager to do" (Gal. 2:10, niv). As a people who reflect our Father's heart, helping the poor should also be a main concern of ours, which is an open door of opportunity to prove our faith by good works.

Paul was so concerned with the poverty amongst the Jerusalem church that it led to faith in action. He organized a collection to meet their needs (1 Cor. 16:1–2). Good works through faith include financially supporting those who work for the gospel, too. In 1 Corinthians 9:14 we are reminded that "the Lord has commanded that those who preach the gospel should receive their living from the gospel" (NIV), so donating to the collection at church not out of obligation but cheerfully, as if giving to the Lord, is also a way to serve.

Supporting charities that help the poor in different ways is another good way to show faith in action, although each one of us is responsible to find out if the charities we choose to support are trustworthy and honest. Giving to beggars and the homeless on the street also brings glory to God, but it is often better to buy something they need, such as a sandwich or clothing, because they may use the money to purchase something that will do them more harm than good.

Organizing or participating in a church outreach, such as clearing up a poor neighborhood, is also an example of a good work through faith in God. This could consist of helping with gardening for private households and public pathways and parks, clearing disused areas, and even preaching the gospel in those communities.

Smaller-scale ideas include helping the elderly with their shopping and volunteering to lend a hand to someone with physical disabilities by assisting them with their housework, walking their dog, or reading to them. Offering lifts if you have a car, volunteering to help out at a charity or benevolent organization, and generally always being generous and kind to strangers are all excellent ways to serve.

The Bible exhorts us to be hospitable and share meals with people (Luke 14:12–14; Acts 2:46–47). (See the section entitled "Hospitality" in Chapter 4.) John emphasizes the importance of looking after traveling teachers in 3 John 5.

To sum up this section, proving the authenticity of our faith by good works involves an activity in which our faith moves us to action through our genuine concern for someone else's welfare. Jesus challenges us that these good deeds especially need to be carried out to strangers and enemies. We should expect nothing in return.

> And if you do good to those who do good to you, what credit is that to you? For even sinners do the same.
>
> —LUKE 6:33

Jesus gives us some extra guidelines with regard to our works through faith:

> Take heed that you do not do your charitable deeds before men, to be seen by them. Otherwise you have no reward from your Father in heaven. Therefore, when you do a charitable deed, do not sound a trumpet before you as the hypocrites do in the synagogues and in the streets, that they may have glory from men. Assuredly, I say to you, they have their reward. But when you do a charitable deed, do not let your left hand know what your right hand is doing, that your charitable deed may be in secret; and your Father who sees in secret will Himself reward you openly.
>
> —MATTHEW 6:1–4

We learn from this that we should not announce our works, just carry them out quietly and humbly with the knowledge that God knows our thoughts and actions.

If you are in a situation in which you are surrounded by people who need to see your light because they do not have the light of Christ in them, Jesus gives us different instructions: "Nor do they light a lamp and put it under a basket, but on a lampstand, and it gives light to all who are in the house. Let your light so shine before men, that they may see your good works and glorify your Father in heaven" (Matt. 5:15–16). To whomever you are witnessing, allow such people to see your deeds, but hide them from those who already have the love of Christ in them in order to receive the full reward.

One snare the devil has laid is the belief that intentions are sufficient. If we intend to do good but never do it, we seem to think that that is enough, because God knows what we think. However, it will not be counted before God as if we had done it. We have to actually carry out the good deed. We need to be aware that Jesus is coming soon and will repay people according to their deeds, as recorded in Revelation 22:12. He will not repay us in proportion to our good intentions but rather what our good works are and how we carry them out.

HOPE

> For whatever things were written before were written for our learning, that we through the patience and comfort of the Scriptures might have hope.
>
> —ROMANS 15:4

The world is searching for hope—hope for their illnesses, hope for their children, hope for success, hope for longevity, hope to realize their dreams. Sometimes they put their hope in their own ability, charms, other people, or luck, to name a few. God's Word tells us that "heaven and earth will pass away, but My words will by no means pass away" (Matt. 24:35). If all these things will disappear, with just one thing remaining, we need to put our hope in it and in the one who gave it to us.

Living with our hope in God and His Word is living by the belief that without Him in our life we are worth nothing and that everything we do, if it doesn't have God's signature under it, is worthless. When God is our only hope, our perspective on life becomes radically different than other people's; we are firmly convicted that we depend on God for everything and know that if we try to achieve anything by our own strength, it is useless. This hope enables us to look toward the future with complete trust in God's grace.

A large part of living with hope is believing God for life after death. This hope removes any fear of dying, as we know with all our heart where we will go if we remain in Jesus and we trust that place is more wonderful than Earth, free of problems and tears (Rev. 7:16–17). Such hope serves to spur us on; it gives us something to look forward to. Just as a worker's motivation to do a good job for his employer is his pay, we will receive our main salary when we leave this life.

> For we know that if our earthly house, this tent, is destroyed, we have a building from God, a house not made with hands, eternal in the heavens.
>
> —2 CORINTHIANS 5:1

The only one who can give us this hope is the Holy Spirit, as Paul goes on to say in verse 5: "As a guarantee he has given us his Holy Spirit" (NLT). This hope implies confident expectation, completely trusting in God (Rom. 15:13), not just want and belief.

In Luke 8:41–56 Jairus, the leader of the synagogue, had just received news of his only daughter's death. He probably felt despair, desperation, and intense sadness. His hope had died along with his daughter. Jesus says to anyone facing the same type of hopelessness as Jairus did, "Fear not: believe only" in verse 50 (KJV). Jairus couldn't see or imagine any reason to just believe after receiving such shocking news, but with those simple instructions Jesus gave him hope and faith in what seemed impossible. Jesus then visited Jairus's home and spoke strong words to the young girl: "Maid, arise" (Luke 8:54, KJV). The voice of the Creator, who said, "Let there be light," also speaks this to our hope, breathing new life into it.

As our hope arises, the Word of God calls us to wait on Him in eager expectancy as He provides for our needs, both physical and spiritual. At the same time, as we put our hope in Christ's words, we patiently await our salvation and expect to witness the fulfillment of His promises. Waiting on God for Him to do these things blesses us (Isa. 30:18) and gives rest to our souls (Ps. 62:5).

We are given this hope of forgiveness and redemption by the Holy Spirit, which manifests itself in acts of love carried out by faith (Gal. 5:5–6). The hope within us assures us of our glorious future with the Lord and therefore wells over into joy and inexhaustible love toward God and those around us. This love in action is carried out by faith, so a three-point circle of faith, hope, and love is functioning within Christians. It starts with hope (Col. 1:5), although hope alone does not save us; faith does that.

Sometimes we are in desperate need of comfort and hope under the worst possible circumstances, especially when it seems like nothing is going right. We keep hitting a brick wall, and God appears to be silent. In times such as these, we can only base our hope on who God is. He who is just and all-powerful allows things for a reason and does not delay His intervention in vain. Sometimes God's silence is a way of testing us. He is also a forgiving God, who does not remain angry forever. We need to constantly reflect on Him and His attributes; in turn, He will fill our hearts with His hope and truth. As we patiently wait on Him to do this, as the psalmist suggests in Psalm 37:7, He will fill us with strength (Isa. 40:31) and enable us to accept our grief. Remember Job's suffering and trials. Through all his anguish, he never allowed his hope to be smashed (Job 19:25–27). Peter's advice to those suffering trials is to rejoice in the hope of our eternal inheritance in heaven and God's protective power over us (1 Pet. 1:3–6).

Mephibosheth, the grandson of Saul, had more than enough troubles of his own. Crippled in both feet from the age of five, he had lost all of his close blood relatives on his father's side. Because the Bible tells us he lived in the house of someone else, he was probably poor, with few possessions. He was the grandson of a deceased king and yet described himself as a "dead dog" (2 Sam. 9:8). When David inquired of Ziba if Saul had any surviving relatives, instead of saying Mephibosheth's name, Ziba focused on his disability. Mephibosheth's identity was caught up in his hindrance; Mephibosheth was presumably often treated this way throughout life.

However, when he was presented before David, instead of focusing on his problem, the king called him by his name (2 Sam. 9:6) and gave him great honor and riches. In the same way, when we feel poor in spirit and like a dead dog, God calls us by name and revives our hope. He doesn't look at our problem as Ziba did but welcomes us as an honored guest and restores our spiritual riches. Mephibosheth's life was completely turned around in a day. His hope was renewed, and he prospered beyond what he could ever have imagined. Mephibosheth may have grown weary from his predicament and all his misfortune, but his hope passed the test.

Chapter 4

FRUITS AND GIFTS OF THE SPIRIT

And it shall come to pass afterward, that I will pour out my spirit upon all flesh; and your sons and your daughters shall prophesy, your old men shall dream dreams, your young men shall see visions: and also upon the servants and upon the handmaids in those days will I pour out my spirit.

JOEL 2:28–29, KJV

W E ARE LIVING after the first coming of the Messiah, in which there is a special time of outpouring of the Spirit of God, enabling and equipping His people in holiness and righteousness and additionally producing gifts, such as dreams and prophecies. The Holy Spirit is given freely and abundantly to those who put their faith and life in Jesus' hands and who live obediently and submissively to God. This pouring out, mentioned in Joel 2:29, refers to the Holy Spirit generously drenching the receiver with God's righteousness, peace, and joy (Rom. 14:17) until overflowing, just as the vats overflow with wine in Joel 2:24. Isaiah's prophecy concerning the overflow of the Holy Spirit on God's people looks upon the present time as a period of enjoyment, fertility, spiritual success, peace, obedience, and fruitfulness never experienced by Israel before (Isa. 32:15–20).

The Spirit is the part of God who is present on the earth (Ps. 139:7), while the Father and Son are in heaven. It is by Him God imparts to us a new heart and a new spirit as we are born again, and He empowers us to be obedient to Him (Ezek. 36:26–27). The Spirit of God was hovering over the waters at Creation (Gen. 1:2), and yet He also lives in people (John 14:17). He gives the breath of life (Job 33:4), and yet He convicts the world of sin, righteousness, and judgement (John 16:8). He acts as a seal in us as a deposit of our eternal life and inheritance (2 Cor. 1:22).

Receiving the Holy Spirit begins with His baptism, first directly introduced in the Scriptures in Matthew 3:11, where John the Baptist declares that Jesus "shall baptize you with the Holy Ghost, and with fire" (KJV). The fire John prophesies about refers to the believer being "set on fire for God." Through the new presence of the Holy Spirit in our lives, we receive spiritual power and start to run the Christian race with all our strength and being, where all we desire to do is for God. We have a new urge to give our all to the Lord and to walk in His ways with all our hearts. Jeremiah describes this fire as something he cannot hold in. The fire within compels him to spread God's Word (Jer. 20:9). Peter and John found God's all-consuming fire had the same effect on them. They said, "For we cannot but speak the things which we have seen and heard" (Acts 4:20, KJV). God's cleansing and refining fire completely transforms the believer.

The baptism of the Holy Spirit is simply the first time the Holy Spirit comes upon us. He can manifest Himself in various forms. For some, it is by an amazing and serene peace upon people and the knowledge their sins are forgiven; hence, they are made right with God. This knowledge of God's love often draws people to tears. With others, He manifests Himself by giving them the gift of speaking an unlearned language, called "tongues" in the Bible, and prophesying, which is what happened to twelve men in Acts 19:6 when Paul laid his hands on them.

After the initial baptism of the Spirit, the Christian is then filled with the Spirit (Eph. 5:18, KJV). The Holy Spirit inside the person is described as "rivers of living water" that flow from within (John 7:38, KJV). Due to this effect of fresh cleansing inside, Jesus also declares that the person will never feel spiritual thirst again (John 4:14).

The Holy Spirit within authorizes us to speak the Word of God with boldness (Acts 4:31), and He fills us with joy (Acts 13:52). The filling of the Holy Spirit referred to in these references in Acts does not suggest a one-time experience. Instead, as the passages are written in the present tense, it is to continually take place. The fellowship with the Holy Spirit is essential in the lives of each believer (2 Cor. 13:14), and we must always be controlled by His influence (Rom. 8:9). The fire inside us must be kept burning continually, just as the fire on the altar in Leviticus 6:12–13 was never allowed to go out.

Simeon, a man who dedicated most of his life to walking in the Spirit, had such intimacy with Him that the Spirit of God revealed he would see Israel's Redeemer (Luke 2:26). Obedient to the Spirit, we can presume he went wherever the Holy Spirit led him, as a vessel in God's hand. He prophesied over baby Jesus' and Mary's future suffering, as the Lord guided him.

The automatic consequence of living in obedience to God's will and in the fellowship of the Holy Spirit is bearing spiritual fruit. When we are born again, a character transformation takes place in our old, sinful selves and we become a new creation and lead a new life (1 Cor. 5:17). Through the sanctification of the Holy Spirit in our lives, we progress toward being people who possess a blameless temperament, which is constituted of the following fruits: "love, joy, peace, longsuffering, kindness, goodness, faithfulness, gentleness, self-control" (Gal. 5:22–23) and "righteousness" (Philippians 1:11). (See Chapter 11, "Righteous Living.")

The yielding of these fruits is natural in a repentant heart (Matt. 3:8), but it is important to note that if we strive to engender such character traits on our own without being born again, we will fail. Jesus tells us in John 15:4 that anyone who produces such fruit cannot do so on their own; it is only through His saving power that we generate these characteristics. It is also possible, however, to backslide and stop producing them. Therefore, we must be careful to remain in Him.

> Abide in Me, and I in you. As the branch cannot bear fruit of itself, unless it abides in the vine, neither can you, unless you abide in Me.
>
> —JOHN 15:4

Light enables fruit trees to produce organic substances from water and carbon dioxide, which in turn generate growth so they produce the crop. Light is their source of energy. Knowledge of God's glory through Christ is our light and source of spiritual energy (2 Cor. 4:6), because, mixed with other ingredients such as His presence and Word, we too grow and turn out fruit.

As a consequence of bearing good fruit for Jesus, He authorizes us to ask for things in prayer in His name. In general, we place too much emphasis on asking for things in the name of Jesus, without paying attention to what He says. This is why many people find their prayers go unanswered. Only after bearing good fruit will the Father give us whatever we ask for in Jesus' name. Notice the position of the word *then* in John 15:16: "I chose you and appointed you to go and bear fruit—fruit that will last. Then the Father will give you whatever you ask in my name " (NIV).

It is common knowledge that edible fruit from the ground is sweet, juicy, and tasty, containing seeds that eventually produce even more. God also made fruit to be colorful and healthy to eat, full of vitamins and goodness; not fattening but energizing. These natural features reflect how spiritual fruit benefits our soul. Instead of being physically healthy and beautiful to the eye, holy fruit gives health and vibrancy to the soul, providing rest and restoration to our minds as we produce them. Whenever we demonstrate kindness and humility, compassion and gentleness toward people, our soul becomes energized and revitalized. Yielding this fruit is the desire God gave to our inner being when He made us, so when we do not bear pure fruit, our souls become sick and our desires twisted. The seeds within fruit symbolize prospective children in the faith, that is, people who become Christians through our witness.

Anyone who claims to be a Christian yet does not produce these fruits of the Spirit is actually not. We will always be able to tell who is really saved by the fruit they bear rather than by what they say they are, although we have not been given the right to judge anyone. In Matthew 7:19–20, Jesus says, "Every tree that does not bear good fruit is cut down and thrown into the fire. Therefore by their fruits you will know them." Of course, if someone dies straight after becoming a Christian and therefore does not have time to demonstrate such fruit, they will still be saved on resurrection day.

Jesus is the true Vine, our source, who makes bearing fruit attainable. It is not us but Jesus who makes it possible (John 15:5). God wants fruit twenty-four–seven, not just on Sunday at church, which is why we need to constantly walk in the Holy Spirit, with our spirit connected to Him in praise and prayer in order for Him to work in us to yield fruit. The Farmer loves the Vine, and He loves those of us who are in the Vine. He desires us to produce fruit for Him, and if we don't, we will be rejected as worthless (John 15:6). When we do bear fruit, Jesus warns that we will be pruned to become even more fruitful (John 15:2). This is God's way of saying that our patience, humility, kindness, and compassion are strengthened under suffering (Rom. 5:3–4).

The patience referred to here is the kind of patience that allows us to wait or persist quietly without retaliating, objecting, or gossiping about the situation at hand, displaying self-control and humility. Jesus proved His divine patience on the cross when, although heckled, laughed at, and tempted to prove His power, He cried out to God to forgive His enemies of their ignorance (Luke 23:34). He did not strike back or return any accusations or judgment, which was His right as God. Instead, like a lamb going to slaughter, He silently endured fatal brutality.

In the same manner, following Jesus' perfect example, each believer must sustain patience in human relationships. This can sometimes be a challenge, especially with our unbelieving and also believing family members. In all we do, we must be calm and loving, giving tolerant and gentle replies to all questions and subjects raised. We should avoid snappy reactions or remarks and be gracious and sympathetic when someone is slower to learn or catch on to an idea or concept, always being careful not to make fun. Our patience and gentleness should be such within relationships so that when someone cries, we cry with them. When they suffer, we suffer along with them.

Another challenging area where Christians should shine out as a composed and mild-tempered people is in traffic. We should be courteous toward all other drivers, driving wisely and with utmost caution. Only use the horn when really necessary to warn someone of danger, and always be ready to turn the other cheek when someone pushes into a line or disrespects you.

Likewise, we must have the attitude of Christ and His meekness when waiting in a line. In the supermarket, bank, and restaurant, we must show patient restraint with the cashier and employees. We must remain dressed with the humility and tenderness of Jesus Christ. We should prove our kindness and gentleness through our loving attitude and forbearance, always putting others first. When we are mistreated or have been overlooked by someone, for instance, we need to accept the situation and not fight for our rights or demand justice. Our justice comes from God, so we must humbly accept such situations and treat everyone with goodness, regardless of whether we think they deserve it or not.

In the face of someone sinning against us, we must be full of unfailing forgiveness, no matter how many times our pardon is required (Matt. 18:22). Just as God is patient, graceful, and merciful to us to forgive our sins, so we should forgive other people who offend us. If we don't, how can we expect to receive God's forgiveness and eternal life? God is patient with us to repent (Rom. 2:4), so we should be faithful to everyone else.

The New King James Version of Colossians 3:12 uses *longsuffering* instead of *patience*. This concerns patient endurance of affliction and tribulation. (See the section entitled "Endurance in Suffering" in Chapter 13.)

As we present our requests to God in prayer, we also need to display persistence while we wait for God to act on our behalf (Ps. 37:7). Composure and forbearance are required while we wait for our prayers to be answered, for example, to see loved ones saved, for revival, for relief from a problem, or for God's promises to be fulfilled in our lives. Similarly, as we look to God for direction in our lives, we must have a confident, unhurried attitude while we anticipate His intervention (Ps. 25:5), not forgetting that humility and the fear of the Lord are needed for this (vv. 9, 12).

The Bible also talks about the patience Christians need in the faith to stand firm and persevere until Jesus' second coming (James 5:7–8). (See the section entitled "Perseverance" in Chapter 13.)

JOY

Rejoice in the Lord always: and again I say, Rejoice.
—PHILIPPIANS 4:4, KJV

The first reason for Christians to rejoice is the Lord. As the Holy Spirit witnesses to our spirits that Jesus Christ is Lord (John 15:26), just knowing and realizing what He has done for us, His incredible love and favor on us, who He is, and His dedication and deep care for us is a reason to celebrate with gladness and cheer. As we grow in knowledge, we will come to a deeper realization of God's majesty and might, as well as His sovereignty and eternal glory. As He leads us into this revelation of His righteousness, faithfulness, fatherly love, grace, and holiness, the fact that He chooses to pour His love and mercy on us takes us into even deeper awe, humility, and joy. God's provision in our lives, including the creation of the earth, which He designed for us to live in and made beautiful for us to enjoy, is an expression of His wisdom and ingenuity. The fact that the same being is our loving Father who provides for us is motive for true delight.

Biblical joy is often expressed together with praise, which is manifest as dancing, shouting, creative writing and speech, the clapping of hands, music, and singing. David found basis for much celebration and joy when the ark of the covenant was transferred to Jerusalem. He ordered the Levites to sing upbeat songs and play a variety of instruments (1 Chron. 15:16). He was commemorating God's nearness and personal care for His people because of the Israelites' victory in finally receiving the ark of the Lord in its proper place, Zion. David's joy was such that he publicly danced and jumped around (2 Sam. 6:16), causing his wife to scorn him. The joy his spirit displayed is the kind of joyfulness spiritual breakthrough and victory bring to those who have been faithfully praying for and awaiting it.

The gladness the Holy Spirit brings us is also due to other aspects in the Christian life. God's wonderful gift of salvation; the fact that we have been forgiven and are undeservedly made right before God, and therefore have our hope set on an eternal inheritance awaiting us in heaven is cause for real jubilation (1 Pet. 1:3–8; Rom. 12:12). The psalmist expresses this joy in Psalm 98 by calling the whole earth and its inhabitants to rush forth into an outburst of joyful singing, celebrating our deliverance. The call to clap and chant extends even to the earth's inanimate features, as they have eagerly been awaiting God's salvation since man's rebellion in Genesis 3.

It is a spiritual law that the righteous are joyous. As we lead a life characterized by our morals, the Holy Spirit will pour out His joy upon us (Ps. 97:11–12). This inner satisfaction is a fruit of being free from sin. Sin in its destructive nature attacks our emotions negatively. As a blameless people, we are free from such assaults, which gives way for the Holy Spirit to freely fill us with His spiritual exuberance and bliss.

This is a part of our reward here on Earth that goes much deeper than simply having a good sense of humor and laughing often; rather, it is a certainty given us that we are sealed by God's love. This joy exists in our inner being and manifests itself subtly in our everyday attitudes when we are a worry-free people, fully trusting in our Savior. It is closely linked to the peace Jesus has left us (John 14:27), because this wonderful joy is unable to exist in those who do not have Jesus' peacefulness. The two exist side-by-side as fruits of the Spirit.

As children of the Most High, we should expect seasons of difficulty, temptation, and testing. As we trust in the Lord and fight for victory, when that moment arrives, joy will fill our hearts. Psalm 30 is a wonderful demonstration of this process. The joy wells up to such an extent inside David that he pledges to thank God forever (v. 12). The joy of the Lord causes David to become energetic and noisy in his expression of praise and thanksgiving. David's victory over his enemies is the same for us today too when God rescues us from sticky or uncomfortable situations and heals us from our illnesses. When we feel the great burden lifting from our shoulders, it is joy and thanksgiving that flood our heart. In consequence of the delight that deluged David's heart when God set him free from his troubles, he could not help but concentrate on the Lord's justice, righteousness, and fame (Ps. 9:7–12).

The Holy Spirit causes us to have inner joy even in the face of difficulties and suffering due to the gospel of Jesus Christ as we remember our reward (Matt. 5:11–12) and how our faith will mature through hard times (James 1:2). Peter reminds his readers that the only attitude to have while in distress due to persecution of the faith is that of inner contentment because we share in His glory and God is on our side (1 Pet. 4:13–14).

Paul found he not only had inexpressible pleasure because of suffering for Christ (2 Cor. 12:10), but also he felt indescribable joy over his converts (1 Thess. 2:19–20). The work of an evangelist, when he sees fruit and God's hand on what he does, is a reason for true delight. In Romans 10:15, Paul celebrates the fact that his feet are called "beautiful" by the prophet Isaiah.

The humble and needy are the type of people who have the most reason to rejoice. This is because they cannot trust in riches or material goods; rather, they have to trust in the Lord, who is their watcher and helper. Mary realizes that because her humility has been seen by God, He has allowed her to rejoice in Him through His blessings (Luke 1:47–49). God stretches out His hand to help the humble and poor because they recognize they need Him, and so receive His help, which in turn causes satisfaction and gladness (Isa. 29:19).

The only way to feel joyful is through God giving joy to us. He is our faithful and just Provider, so no matter how much we try to find this biblical and penetrating bliss on our own, we will fail. It is a special and sacred reward the Holy Spirit gives only to those who are faithful and obedient to Himself.

PEACE

Let the peace of Christ rule in your hearts, since as members of one body you were called to peace.

—COLOSSIANS 3:15, NIV

The peace that God gives goes beyond all understanding and viable explanation. It is a present that God has decided to leave His people to reassure them of their salvation (Rom. 8:6). It is a supernatural feeling which anyone who does not trust and obey Christ will ever be able to feel. It is an inner serenity that takes away anxiety and fear (John 14:27). It is greater and more profound than what any religion, philosophy, or meditation can ever bring anyone. It is only possible for the Creator of human beings to bestow this peace because He made us in such a way that our soul craves it. Everybody's soul yearns for peace with God, although the majority does not realize their need. Others resort to searching to try and find it in music, material possessions, love, sex, work, or academic achievements; but without looking to the cross, they will never encounter what is probably their greatest spiritual need, after love.

This peace protects us from mental conflict and gives us stable mental health. It annuls demonic oppression manifested as anger, distress, strain, vexation, anguish, and cerebral torment, by renewing and refreshing the mind. It provides us with a real sense of security (Ps. 112:8). Peace also confirms our identity in Christ, because Jesus brought it to us and He Himself is our peace (Eph. 2:14).

His peace does not mean we will never have any problems or worries; rather, it will sustain and protect us when difficulties arise. There will be conflicts and battles in this life, but the peace of God's presence guides us through them. If we trust in God for safety, He will even give us peaceful sleep (Ps. 4:8).

As Christians, we can sometimes interrupt this peaceable feeling. We are not at peace with God when we sin, or when we allow negative, evil, and destructive thoughts and images to occupy our minds and imaginations. This may be by imagining ill-fated happenings or viewing unfortunate, gory, crude, or offensive situations and pictures. Just observing unholy things and creating evil desires within us separates us from God's peace. It is very easy to sin just by using our imaginations. But our imaginations can also be used to bring us closer to God, such as using it to plan for the future, to plan to read the Bible in six months, or how to reach out to friends. We need to learn to control our creative thinking. Essentially, any sin and even thoughts about sinning and shameful things separate us from God's peace, which is why Paul instructs us to think about "whatever is true, whatever is noble, whatever is right, whatever is pure, whatever is lovely, whatever is admirable…anything…excellent or praiseworthy" (Philippians 4:8, NIV) in order for God to sanctify us. In the same way, doing good cures us from spiritual illnesses and brings us inner tranquility (Rom. 2:10) as the Holy Spirit floods our hearts.

In order to keep God's peace within, think about Him and trust in Him always (Isa. 26:3) and allow His peace to "rule in your hearts" (Col. 3:15, NIV). From Isaiah 48:18, we can see that we gain God's peace by obedience to His commands, so we must make sure we are living in complete submission to His Word. We ought to seek God for His direction in life, walk in it, and our souls will be at rest (Jer. 6:16).

Justification through faith brings us peace with God (Rom. 5:1). The peace referred to in Romans 5:1 not only refers to the peace described above but also to being able to stand before God without the stain of sin. We therefore now have access to a relationship with Him. Peace is the essence of the gospel message (Acts 10:36) because we are at peace with God through Christ's redemptive work (Eph. 2:14–18).

In addition to the subjective feeling that God's peace of mind brings us, peace in the Bible also refers to the state of peace and unity among believers (Eph. 4:3) and all men (Heb. 12:14). The Bible commands us to try our hardest to live at peace with everyone (Rom. 14:19). Jesus specifically directs us to resolve conflict before it gets out of hand and especially before sacrificing to God (Matt. 5:23–25).

Christians are called to be peacemakers (Matt. 5:9), and in order for us to fulfill our vocation, the Bible gives many hints and practical advice. Gentleness and a calm attitude sow peace (Prov. 15:1). Even presenting gifts to pacify someone works, as Proverbs 21:14 tells us. Jacob used this tactic to cool his brother's possible wrath (Gen. 32:20–21). Paul encourages the Thessalonians to conduct themselves collectedly and modestly (1 Thess. 4:11), and he reminds Titus that the people (us) should be obedient to authorities, not gossip, and be humble in order to keep the peace (Titus 3:1–2).

Abraham is a biblical figure who resorted to a diplomatic and sensible solution in order to pacify the land. As a result of quarreling between his and Lot's herdsmen, probably over land usage, he came to the practical solution of separating them from one another, but he wisely and unselfishly gave Lot the first choice of land (Gen. 13:9). We too should always be quick to soothe relations and be democratic about keeping the peace with everybody. In order to do this, we must always give others first choice so they will have nothing to accuse us of later.

Jesus says He actually came to the earth not to bring peace, but division, even amongst immediate members of a family (Luke 12:51–53). At first this may seem like a contradiction to other references about Jesus and the peace He leaves His people, but in fact, He is expressing the conflict He has brought between the church and the world. The devil's kingdom cannot accept believers for who they are because there is no light in the world, and darkness hides from the light so as not to expose its evil deeds. This causes friction between God's and Satan's people, who can belong to the same nuclear family. In the spiritual realm, the non-Christian member of the family is in a spiritual war against the Christian, and vice-versa (2 Cor. 6:14–15), whether this is apparent or not.

MERCY AND COMPASSION

> He who oppresses the poor shows contempt for their Maker, but whoever is kind to the needy honors God.
>
> —PROVERBS 14:31, NIV

God created the rich and the poor, the good and the bad, the weak and the strong, the sick and the healthy in His own image, sending rain and sunshine on all. In the same way, when we are kindhearted toward the poor, the sick, the weak, and the evil by sharing with them and showing them loving-kindness, we imitate God and act in fear of Him. God stresses the importance of being charitable and humane to those who least deserve it by prioritizing it amongst His requirements in Micah 6:8: "He has shown you, O man, what is good; And what does the LORD require of you But to do justly, To love mercy, And to walk humbly with your God?" God's own perfect example of demonstrating mercy is the sending of His only Son to die on the cross for us, disobedient sinners who are unworthy.

The central and most shocking part of Jesus' Sermon on the Mount was instructing the crowd to love their enemies, bless those who curse them, and pray for whoever abuses them. The heart of this seemingly upside-down teaching is proving one's love for others by displaying mercy and compassion toward those who mistreat us. Jesus not only taught not to retaliate and get angry toward anyone but to actually express affection to everyone, especially when they are least deserving from a human point of view.

The nearest thing many of us generally have nowadays as a human enemy is that person we never see eye to eye with. Sometimes we are in the same social circle as them, and other times they are someone we bump in to occasionally, someone at work, or even a family member. Instead of regretting their presence in our lives, we should thank God for the opportunity to be able to shine out and be different by purposely acting kindheartedly and neighborly toward them, not just acting but putting our love into action by going out of our way to bless and help them. We need to forgive and forget their past offenses against us, remembering that our time on Earth is momentary and that all we do here will be judged and either counted for or against us.

David had a fierce enemy who was also a family member, his father-in-law, who actively chased him to kill him. Many of us could not claim to have a worse personal enemy than this. When the opportunity arose for David to take revenge upon his enemy of old, he showed loving mercy and prohibited his men from attacking Saul in any way (1 Sam. 24:7). David showed compassion and leniency toward the person who turned his life around and forced him to wander around the wilderness as a nomad, living in fear of his life. What a gracious example for us to follow!

Mercy can also be manifested as compassion, especially toward poor and sick people whom we do not know on a personal level. Sponsoring a child in the third world is a way of showing such clemency, as well as visiting strangers and friends in hospitals and hospices. Being concerned for and providing care for people without families and generally meeting people's needs are examples of how to be sympathetic to one's neighbor. (See Chapters 2 and 3.)

There is a huge bonus to being merciful. If we prove to be compassionate in this life, God will manifest His mercy toward us on the Day of Judgment. In James's words, "Mercy triumphs over judgment" (James 2:13). Also, the Old and the New Testaments both promise blessings for the softhearted in Proverbs 14:21 and Matthew 5:7.

FORGIVENESS

> If another believer sins, rebuke that person; then if there is repentance, forgive. Even if that person wrongs you seven times a day and each time turns again and asks forgiveness, you must forgive.
>
> —LUKE 17:3–4, NLT

An unforgiving spirit is a single characteristic that can cause us to lose our salvation. We may be excelling in all other areas of our faith and walk with God, but if we fail to forgive just one person, it will all be in vain. Jesus says, "For if you forgive men their trespasses, your heavenly Father will also forgive you. But if you do not forgive men their trespasses, neither will your Father forgive your trespasses" (Matt. 6:14). In the parable of the unforgiving debtor, Jesus explains the result of the Lord being unable to pardon our sins: "Then the angry king sent the man to prison to be tortured until he had paid his entire debt" (Matt. 18:34, NLT). God's capacity to forgive our sins depends on our ability to forgive other people.

For Christians, forgiveness is a moral obligation without exception or limit. Just as Jesus forgives us our sins when we are repentant, we should forgive others (Luke 6:37). Forgiveness is also the key for the restoration of a hurting soul, relieving the weight of sin and guilt.

It can be very difficult to describe the psychological agony caused by certain offenses, especially that of betrayal by a friend, spouse, or family member, because of the sheer depth of the pain, especially when committed by someone we trusted. Sometimes our will inside us does not want to forgive. Grudges and firm feelings of unforgiveness can take over our hearts, which make us feel rotten as the Holy Spirit departs. We often think that the person who offended us must be punished. Without self-control over our minds, it can be very easy to allow our imaginations to become overactive. After the offense has been committed, we often find ourselves recalling the moment of the misdemeanor over and over again, imagining different reactions and inventing new defenses we could have used.

Another error is questioning the wrongdoer, trying to find reasons, motives, and explanations. Such inquiring and speculation allow harsher feelings to fester, building a fortress inside the mind. Soon it will be such a stronghold that it will be harder and harder to break, and therefore much more difficult to forgive. We need to be vigilant so as to not let our thoughts take over us, and with restraint, each time we feel such thinking creep up, we need to actively tell ourselves that we are not going to contemplate it anymore. We should not ask questions of the insulter, nor should we humiliate, manipulate, or abuse them; but rather, we ought to respect and love them.

Remember that some offenses are not offenses at all, just misunderstandings that have been blown out of proportion. Therefore put yourself in the other person's shoes and try and think of his defense. Maybe you misread his sign or words, or maybe his culture is different and what he did is acceptable according to his background.

Courage is needed to make the decision to excuse them. Resolving to forgive someone takes place inside our spirits and is a step of faith. Forgiveness is a choice, not a feeling. When we forgive and forget, it heals and restores our spiritual wound. The Holy Spirit will then saturate us with love and peace. When we live in the Spirit, we are able forgive; but when we walk in the flesh, it is much harder.

True forgiveness does not demand an explanation, put requirements on the person, nor tell the town about what happened. It also stops mentioning the resentment and is able to face the person. It does not play mind games with the offender, threaten them, or demand compensation. When real exoneration has taken place, seeing the person blessed makes us truly happy. The weight of vengeance, anger, and hatred, will disappear. Our soul returns to its natural state of tranquility and peace. It is no longer tormented by unforgiveness but feels freedom and alleviation. Forgiveness cures the soul and is one of the greatest expressions of love.

When we really forgive our offender, we too will then repent of any sin we committed during our period of unforgiveness. Sometimes this penitence can include an act to prove to ourselves and to God that we have actually forgiven, such as writing a letter to the person in question or carrying out an act of selflessness toward them. True absolution often causes us to pray for blessings and good things in the forgiven offender's life.

Forgiveness can also be a process and a struggle, especially when someone close to us has hurt us. Often we find we need to repeatedly take the step to pardon the person. When harsh sentiments build up against them again, after we already forgave, we need to forgive again. This may need to be done at first several times a day, for instance; then it may only be necessary a few times a week, then once a month, then once every six months for example, until we have completely managed to let go.

The sons of Jacob were bursting over with bitterness and jealousy toward their father's favorite and spoiled son, Joseph. Unfortunately, he naïvely pushed them over the top by disclosing two of his dreams to them, in which they were all bowing down to him. This made them all the more full of rage and hatred, which inspired them to recklessly sell Joseph into slavery. How would you feel toward your brothers if they did that to you? Then, just when things had started looking up for Joseph in Egypt, he was unjustly thrown into prison for over two years.

Faced with his brothers probably two decades later, Joseph dealt with them in a curious way, probably because he was unable to master his newly opened emotional scars, inflicted by their past treatment of him. He often wailed loudly and uncontrollably after they reentered his life (Gen. 43:30; 45:2; 45:14–15).

Forgiveness is not an easy process, especially amongst brotherly feuds. Joseph's hurt was firmly fixed and caused him to play a number of games with his brothers, which aroused in them emotions of guilt and fear. The struggle within Joseph was that of love versus hate and forgiveness versus harshness. Only when his brothers had suffered false accusations, imprisonment, dread, confusion, and humiliation at Joseph's hand was he able to reveal his true identity to them and hug, kiss, and weep over them. His forgiveness was strained and undertook a long, complicated process to reach full fruition. When this did happen in Genesis 45:4–5, he was able to recognize that all the injustice he suffered happened for the greater good, handcrafted by God. This was the key to his pardoning them, trusting in the Lord to overcome evil with good.

This is also fundamental in helping us forgive those who have upset us—seeing how God has used and can use the situation for good in our and their lives. God is much greater and more powerful than any situation that has caused us resentment.

In a sense, the true story of Joseph allegorizes the coming of Jesus Christ. Joseph's wrestle with forgiveness is illustrated with Christ's victorious struggle with sin, which resulted in His death on the cross and the forgiveness of many. In both cases, one man is sent to save his family, and both were rejected and despised by the ones they were to save. Joseph's life points to the ultimate act of forgiveness in all human history—God's mass forgiving of man's sin. As we are blessed by God's forgiveness, we need to bless those who wrong and sin against us.

John 20:23—"If you forgive anyone his sins, they are forgiven; if you do not forgive them, they are not forgiven" (NIV)—can sometimes cause confusion, although it need not. Some have perverted the original text into an excuse not to forgive. What I believe it actually means is that the power invested in us to proclaim the good news of Christ's forgiveness leads to people either being forgiven of their sins by God if they believe it, or to their condemnation if they do not.

Hospitality

> When God's people are in need, be ready to help them. Always
> be eager to practice hospitality.
>
> —Romans 12:13, nlt

Hospitality is a command in the New Testament and also a natural side
effect of the overflowing love the Holy Spirit has placed in our hearts. No
matter how humble our resources and homes are, we should naturally want
to share what we have with other believers.

Whenever a brother in Christ has a need, it is everyone's responsibility to
help him out. It is very easy to tell someone we'll pray for him, give him a
hug, and be on our way without actually meeting his physical need. But, the
Bible orders us to be ready to meet the needs of God's people and be anxious
to host; after all, we might be obliviously entertaining angels (Heb. 13:2)!

Practicing hospitality is a part of working out our salvation. The Samaritan in the parable of the good Samaritan was merciful and kind by showing
love through his courteousness and sympathy even far from home. Nothing
stopped him from accommodating someone in need, moreover an enemy
and stranger. We, too, need to affirm we're good neighbors by lovingly
receiving and welcoming people wherever we are. Hospitality is a self-sacrificial service demonstrating love in action, which presents the unity of God's
love among His people (3 John 8). Acts 2:46–47 describes the unity in the
Spirit and fellowship among the body of believers through sharing meals.

Jesus' instructions regarding hospitality include accommodating for
those who you know will not be able to pay you back (Luke 14:12–14). This
unselfish act provides us with a reward in the next life. Jesus practiced this
to an extreme by miraculously feeding five thousand and then four thousand men (Mark 6:44; 8:9).

Entertaining guests is actually an important ministry to traveling
evangelists and teachers today. Jesus advised His disciples to accept such
hospitality and gave them specific instructions regarding leaving their
blessing of peace on the givers, accepting whatever food and drink is
set before them, staying in just one house per town (Luke 10:5–9), and

responding when a place is inhospitable (Matt. 10:14; Luke 5:10–11). We need to faithfully administer the talents God has given us, so those with this gift should seek opportunities to spread God's grace in this form. Isaiah 58:7 reminds us of the value of sharing our food with the poor and hungry and dividing our belongings with those who lack them. This brings us an eternal reward (Matt. 25:34–39). Remember, though, we need to entertain guests with wisdom. Second John admonishes against showing hospitality toward false teachers. (See the section entitled "Intolerance of False Christians; Tolerance of Backslidden Christians" in Chapter 8.)

The Shunammite woman in 2 Kings 4 exhibited good cheer and gave a remarkably warm welcome to Elisha by urging him to have a meal (v. 8, NIV). She then perceived his need for accommodation, so she arranged a bedroom for him to freely use in her house (v. 10). Her reward was her greatest desire fulfilled; she gave birth to a son a year later.

UNITY

> Rejoice with those who rejoice, and weep with those who weep. Be of the same mind toward one another. Do not set your mind on high things, but associate with the humble. Do not be wise in your own opinion.
>
> —ROMANS 12:15–16

Through the unity the love of Christ has imparted us, our calling is to share in each other's feelings, sorrows, and possessions (Acts 4:32), showing genuine love and concern. This requires humility and equal favor throughout the church so no one is seen as or treated better or worse than others. Living in harmony does not imply having the same opinion or reaching the same verdict regarding spiritual matters, but agreeing to disagree and putting differences aside and concentrating on the love Jesus has given us. We are summoned to be "like-minded, having the same love, being of one accord, of one mind" (Philippians 2:2). Putting other people and their needs before our own helps develop our like-mindedness, as does demonstrating genuine sympathy, gentleness, and compassion toward everyone. This unity is worked out as living as one with other Christians. Through our oneness with Christ and the common presence of the Holy Spirit in our lives, we are now family with others who have also found forgiveness in Him.

Unfortunately, this is not a perfect world, and we are all still going through the process of sanctification. Some are more advanced along the line than others, so disputes and disagreements can arise. If there is anyone we have had a misunderstanding with or a grudge against, Jesus tells us to quickly, without delay, reconcile ourselves with them: "So if you are presenting a sacrifice at the altar in the Temple and you suddenly remember that someone has something against you, leave your sacrifice there at the altar. Go and be reconciled to that person. Then come and offer your sacrifice to God" (Matt. 5:23–24, NLT).

The underlying message here is that we must always keep our consciences and thoughts in check. We need to be vigilant regarding how we treat and live with other people. If not, God will not accept our sacrifices to Him. The second we notice we have something against an acquaintance, friend, or family member, we must immediately ask his forgiveness for any wrongdoing we have done to him or her, even if we believe we are not the guilty party. When we realize someone has a problem with us, even if it is not our fault, we must still humble ourselves and ask his or her forgiveness, even when we do not understand why he or she is upset or think it is unjustified. In this way, we will be innocent before God.

To live in such a way is a powerful weapon against the kingdom of darkness. In Genesis 4:7, God says to Cain, "If you do well, will you not be accepted? And if you do not do well, sin lies at the door. And its desire is for you, but you should rule over it." From this we can learn that whenever we honor God properly and follow Jesus' advice above, living in harmony and unity with our brothers and always making sure we are reconciled with everyone, we will be sin's master, so it will have no control over us. However, when we choose to wallow in our self-pity and let negative and evil thoughts regarding other people take us over, as it did Cain, who held a grudge against Abel, then sin festers and has a hold over us. Notice God says sin lies at the door; it is always ready to jump up and attempt to dominate our thoughts and actions. We therefore need to be watchful to assure this won't happen, being wise in our relationships with others and resisting the urge to entertain pessimistic and destructive thoughts about them. Instead, "we should help others do what is right and build them up in the Lord. For even Christ didn't live to please himself" (Rom. 15:2–3, NLT).

A major cause of division among Christians is when we hold up church banners.

> Some of you are saying, "I am a follower of Paul." Others are saying, "I follow Apollos," or "I follow Peter," or "I follow only Christ."
>
> —1 CORINTHIANS 1:12, NLT

We have seen exactly the same thing happening transdenominationally today. Some say, "I am from the Assemblies of God;" or, "I am Presbyterian;" or, "I'm a Nazarene;" or, "I'm a Baptist." While it's okay to tell someone what church you belong to if they ask, if you believe Jesus has been raised from the dead for the forgiveness of sins, why preach the name of a church when we should be preaching what Christ has done for us and is doing in us? Jesus must always be our focus, not our denomination, a certain pastor, preacher, or evangelist. We belong to Christ, not to another human or institution, "so don't boast about following a particular human leader" (1 Cor. 3:21, NLT).

We need to fight these divisions as much as possible and be united to the maximum with people from other denominations. "If you want to boast, boast only about the LORD" (1 Cor. 1:31, NLT). Unity is our main weapon against the schemes of the devil upon the church because when Christians and churches unite, there is victory and God is glorified.

SELF-CONTROL

Pursue righteousness, godliness, faith, love, patience, gentleness.

—1 TIMOTHY 6:11

The exhortation to pursue such attributes demonstrates that we need to actively seek them out, which requires effort on our part. This endeavor comes as part of being saved, as we work out our salvation (Philippians

2:12), and is not an optional "extra." We must always seek opportunities to do what is right in a holy way, always remembering our motivation, our love and fear of God. Our love and faith must always blaze before us so people can see that the way we work and function is different from the ways of the world. We must always strive to please everyone with a very rare quality the world respects but rarely exhibits—tenderness.

These pursuits are closely linked to self-control, which must be manifest every single day in the Christian life. In order to obey the above instruction, from 1 Timothy, we need to exercise self-discipline in our eating, drinking, where we look, our thought lives, our desires, and in conversation; allowing our godliness, faith, love, endurance, and gentleness to shine out. We need to be linked up to the Holy Spirit at all times with our minds interconnected with His. Without these personality traits working themselves out in our lives, evil can attack us almost unhindered, as Proverbs 25:28 points out: "Like a city whose walls are broken down is a man who lacks self-control" (NIV).

A way to conform to such qualities is having dominion over our thought life. Paul recognized the significance our thoughts have on our conduct, as he wrote in Philippians 4:8: "Finally, brethren, whatsoever things are true, whatsoever things are honest, whatsoever things are just, whatsoever things are pure, whatsoever things are lovely, whatsoever things are of good report; if there be any virtue, and if there be any praise, think on these things" (KJV). What we meditate upon will be reflected in that which comes out of our mouths and how we occupy our time, so when our thought pattern is blameless and upright, the consequence is pure and saintly behavior.

As we strive with strength of mind to master our thought lives, it is always imperative to bear in mind that such righteous living, although it is part of our salvation and a natural response to God's loving grace, does not earn us God's acceptance. Only through His undeserved mercy are we accepted in His sight, "not because of righteous things we had done" (Titus 3:5, NIV).

More advice to abide by is in Philippians 2:3: "Do nothing out of selfish ambition or vain conceit" (NIV). Not dissimilar to pride, selfish ambition and vain conceit are lethal opponents of equanimity and oneness within the church today. This is a common scheme the devil uses to cause divisions in churches. Selfish ambition, found amongst the works of the flesh listed in Galatians 5:19–20 (NIV), causes us to disregard everyone else's well-being for our own gain. Vain conceit is when we think of ourselves as more important and greater than another person. This is sometimes an easy attitude to slip into when we are with someone who really thinks we are better or more influential than themselves. Of course, we are all of equal value in God's eyes, so these two attitudes are completely deceptive.

Whenever we feel such selfish desires and feelings rising up within, we must apply Paul's counsel in Ephesians 4:22–24: "Put off, concerning your former conduct, the old man which grows corrupt according to the deceitful lusts, and be renewed in the spirit of your mind, and that you put on the new man which was created according to God, in true righteousness and holiness." As new creations in Christ, we must be careful not to give in to the flesh and return to the way we lived before we were enlightened by the gospel of Jesus. Instead, always remember to "present your bodies a living sacrifice, holy, acceptable to God, which is your reasonable service" (Rom. 12:1).

Many Christians seem to forget this calling as they drive or are passengers in a car. They fail to remember that we are called to love our neighbor and pray for those who harm us. If we think we have been mistreated in the road (e.g., if someone pulls out in front of us), we must not forget Jesus' teaching in Matthew 5:22: "But anyone who says, 'You fool!' will be in danger of the fire of hell" (NIV). With a calm and loving attitude, just slow down and carry on as if nothing had happened. Humility and love for one's neighbor is the key to driving with a controlled attitude before a holy God.

We therefore need to be continually cautious with where we take our thoughts, striving to be constantly aware of them and whether they are pleasant before God or not. The Bible also teaches the importance of controlling our eyes and our tongues. (See Chapter 7, "Clean Mouth." Also see the sections entitled "Fleeing from Lustfulness" in Chapter 6 and "Watchfulness" in Chapter 12.)

GIFTS OF THE SPIRIT

> Let love be your highest goal! But you should also desire the special
> abilities the Spirit gives—especially the ability to prophesy.
> —1 CORINTHIANS 14:1, NLT

The gifts the Holy Spirit bestows on us include wisdom, the word of knowledge, faith, healing the sick, performing miracles, prophecy, distinguishing between spirits, tongues, and the interpretation of tongues (1 Cor. 12:4–10). There are many types of other gifts mentioned in the New Testament, such as the gift of serving, teaching, encouraging, generous giving, leading, and showing mercy (Rom. 12:6–8), as well as gifts of administration (1 Cor. 12:28).

The Holy Spirit sometimes imparts these gifts either when the individual is baptized in the Spirit or at a later time in the Christian's life. In all cases, we are each responsible before God to use our spiritual gifts faithfully for His glory (1 Pet. 4:10). As a part of this, we must nurture them (1 Tim. 4:14) and use them in proportion to faith (Rom. 12:6). They serve to benefit the church as a demonstration of God's grace (1 Pet. 4:10) and to strengthen the unity and faith of believers. God uses them to confirm His message of truth to the listeners (Mark 16:20).

Amongst all the gifts, we should foremost desire the gift of prophecy because it edifies the church (1 Cor. 14:12) as well as strengthens, encourages, and comforts the receiver (1 Cor. 14:3), although love is much more important (1 Cor. 13).

Paul had some specific commands regarding the gifts so as to keep order during the church meetings. He says that those who speak in tongues should pray for the gift of their interpretation (1 Cor. 14:13), and when there is a prophecy, its authenticity should be carefully weighed against Scripture (1 Thess. 5:21). Prophets may interrupt the main speaker (1 Cor. 14:30). We should be careful how we treat words of prophecy, because Paul advised the Thessalonians to treat them with respect (1 Thess. 5:20).

Paul clearly states that not everybody receives the gift of tongues (1 Cor. 12:30), contrary to what is often taught today. If someone does not speak in tongues, it does not mean they are not Spirit-filled. Tongues is a controllable gift (1 Cor. 14:32) that is basically praises to God in other languages, whether heavenly or earthly ones (Acts 2:11). Paul tried to calm the Corinthians down regarding this gift, which they presumably thought was the most impressive gift of all.

The healing of diseases and sicknesses is used the most frequently in the Bible as a sign for new converts to believe in the message. Often, we are taught in church to overlook pain and symptoms of illness in order to exercise faith and confess that we have already been cured. This teaching can cause people to say they have been healed when in fact they have not. It is true that Jesus came to restore our spiritual and physical health through His atoning sacrifice, but we still need to look to Him for our healing through faith, instead of using the power of positive thought.

We also need to be aware that performing wonderful miracles and speaking in beautiful tongues in the name of Jesus is not proof of salvation. Jesus informs us that if we do not know Him personally, and He us, despite the manifestation of these gifts of the Spirit we will still go to hell (Matt. 7:21–23).

Chapter 5

HUMILITY

Always be humble and gentle.

<small>Ephesians 4:2, nlt</small>

T HE BIBLE IS very clear in affirming that an essential attribute all Christians should take on is humility. It is repeated again and again in the Old and New Testaments. Just some examples are 2 Chronicles 7:14, Proverbs 6:3, Daniel 10:12, Zephaniah 2:3, James 4:10, and 1 Peter 5:6. God's Word also calls those who are humble, wise: "Who is wise and understanding among you? Let him show it by his good life, by deeds done in the humility that comes from wisdom" (James 3:13, niv).

In order for us as followers of Christ to become humble, we need to find out what the biblical definition of *humility* is. In Philippians 2:3–4, Paul writes, "Let nothing be done through selfish ambition or conceit, but in lowliness of mind let each esteem others better than himself. Let each of you look out not only for his own interests, but also for the interests of others." Paul defines a humble person as someone who puts others before himself in all situations, thinking of others as greater than him. This is also graphically demonstrated in Luke 14 when Jesus advises us to take the lowest place in a banquet rather than try and find the best place high up the table. Even in conversation with other people, we should do this (Philippians 2:4). Humble people are not quick to talk so as to get their opinion in;

rather, they listen to others and wait for their turn to speak. They are more interested in their neighbor than in talking about themselves, a rare quality seen amongst Christians today.

In Isaiah 66:2, we are told, "This is the one I esteem: he who is humble and contrite in spirit, and trembles at my word" (NIV). A contrite spirit is an immediately repentant and sorrowful spirit after sinning. The humility reflected in this verse implies someone who puts God so far before himself that without delay he recognizes when he makes a mistake before Him and is remorseful. He realizes God is so much greater than himself, and he quivers before Him and His Word.

Zephaniah discusses meekness along with humility in Zephaniah 3:12: "I will leave in your midst A meek and humble people, And they shall trust in the name of the LORD." *Meekness* here does not suggest a shy or weak spirit but rather a lowly, modest one. An unpretentious personality automatically helps one to trust in God, because people with this outlook know within themselves they could never get by without His help.

Jesus' humility was phenomenal; just the fact that God took on human flesh and came to Earth, born as a baby in a manger, is something difficult for our minds to really comprehend. Not just that, but He came as a Galilean, the poorest and most despised Israelites of the time. One mind-blowing verse that reflects on Jesus' humility is Zechariah 9:9: "Behold, your King is coming to you; He is just and having salvation, Lowly and riding on a donkey, A colt, the foal of a donkey." Most of us, if we were royalty, would use a BMW or a flashy sports car to enter our capital city triumphantly for one of the last times. Maybe the more humble amongst us would use a Fiat Uno! However, Jesus did not even use His day's equivalent of a Fiat Uno, which would have been a simpler, smaller chariot. He didn't even use a stallion or a horse. He didn't even ride on a donkey. Instead, His choice of transport was a colt! This reflected that He wasn't seeking to draw attention to Himself or to exalt Himself. He wanted all the glory and honor to go to His Father. He didn't want people to focus on a flashy chariot or worldly riches, but rather to concentrate on who God is.

In order for us to be dressed in this humility (Col. 3:12), we need to recognize we are just made of flesh and blood and that God is the almighty Creator of all. Before Him we are insignificant and totally dependent on Him for everything. Think of the grand scheme of things, how many people have lived on Earth since the beginning of time. We are all just tiny specks in a much greater plan. The psalmist hints at the frailty of life in Psalm 78:39, reminding us that we are "but flesh, a passing breeze that does not return" (NIV). Think how much time has passed before God, and how short our lives are in comparison. Pride is so deceitful that it covers up the fragility of life. Life is also so delicate. We depend on Him totally for everything, the air we breathe, water, our health, finances, relationships, and spiritual and material needs. After all, we cannot even turn one of the hairs on our heads white; only He can (Matt. 5:36).

Therefore there is only one reason for Christians to be proud—because of who our Father in heaven is and that in His immense love for us, He sent His one and only Son so we could obtain salvation.

To express just how important humility is in the Christian life, we can take a look at Moses. The Bible says of Moses in Numbers 12:3, "Now Moses was a very humble man, more humble than anyone else on the face of the earth" (NIV). To win the prize for the humblest person in the world, he must have been exceedingly unassuming. The Bible also says in Exodus 33:11, "So the LORD spoke to Moses face to face, as a man speaks to his friend." Without such humility in Moses' life, God would not have had such intimacy with him. Intimacy with God and humility go hand-in-hand. If you want closeness with God, you need to start by being very self-effacing, as Moses was.

Jesus broke the paradigm of every society by declaring:

> But those who exalt themselves will be humbled, and those who humble themselves will be exalted.
>
> —MATTHEW 23:12, NLT

We see this spiritual law put into practice in the parable of the lost son in Luke 15:11–32. The son decides to return to his father only after he suffers pain, hunger, and humiliation, even eating food from the pigs' trough.

Because of this, he is truly humbled and sorry for all the pain he caused his father. When the son lost so much of his pride that he was prepared to offer himself as his father's servant, his father rejoiced and accepted him just as he was, with a changed and repentant heart. (Note the father didn't search to meet the son before modesty entered his son's heart.)

The father in this parable represents God's heart. God is truly pleased with us and welcomes us when we genuinely humble ourselves, although sometimes we may need to go through a painful process to arrive at a truly humbled state of mind, as the son did. Notice that the son represents someone who was a believer, who turned away from God, then got into such a desperate state that his only hope was God, so he became a follower of the Almighty again. This is not someone who never knew God and then came to know him for the first time. It was a backslider who recommitted his life to the Lord.

In our modern society, too, humility is viewed as a weakness and can be despised. In an ironic twist, Jesus uses His humility to draw people to Himself. In Matthew 11:29, He says, "I am gentle and lowly in heart, and you will find rest for your souls." A humble spirit is an essential factor in being a Christian: "For I have come to call not those who think they are righteous, but those who know they are sinners" (Matt. 9:13, NLT). One of the first steps to becoming a Christian is recognizing you are a sinner. To admit that you have made mistakes and do not please God requires humbleness in itself. Those with inflated views of themselves are not called until they lose any self-importance and repent of their haughtiness.

> And the tax collector, standing afar off, would not so much as raise his eyes to heaven, but beat his breast, saying, "God, be merciful to me a sinner!" I tell you, this man went down to his house justified rather than the other; for everyone who exalts himself will be humbled, and he who humbles himself will be exalted.
> —LUKE 18:13–14

Another essential aspect of humility in our lives is submitting without complaining or rebelling to authorities. It can be all too easy to ignore some rules in our land which may seem petty in our eyes but are placed there for a legitimate purpose, such as placing trash in the proper place, returning borrowed items, recycling without cutting corners, and obeying traffic laws and signals. Submission to authorities also entails respecting bosses, policemen, traffic officers, security guards, and customs and immigration officers in airports. The Word of God commands us to do this in Romans 13:1–2, 4:

> Everyone must submit to governing authorities. For all authority comes from God, and those in positions of authority have been placed there by God. So anyone who rebels against authority is rebelling against what God has instituted, and they will be punished.... The authorities are God's servants, sent for your good. (NLT)

As we can see from these verses, all authority has been put in place by God. Jesus even recognized that Pontius Pilate, the man who gave orders for His crucifixion, had received his political influence from God, and Jesus allowed Himself to be subjected to him. So, we should be submissive to them in humility as well.

Christians are also called to be mutually subservient toward one another, "submitting to one another in the fear of God" (Eph. 5:21). (See Chapter 2, "Love," and Chapter 13.)

Jesus reveals that childlikeness, which is similar to humility, is an essential part of the Christian character. He taught that the childlike are accepted by God, not the proud. He prayed, "Thank you for hiding these things from those who think themselves wise and clever, and for revealing them to the childlike" (Matt. 11:25, NLT). A childlike person is not someone who thinks they know it all but someone who recognizes their understanding is lacking, so they listen to God all the more to learn about Him and His ways. They have not allowed opinions and judgments of other people to be developed, so such people are naturally more open to welcoming God's truth with no doubts. Children are not arrogant and proud, nor are they full of hatred and strife or given over to sinful desires. Likewise, we need to be pure and control our attitudes and wants.

Children are 100 percent dependent on their parents and adults to provide for all their needs. In the same way, we must have total dependence on God and rely on Him completely. Childlikeness implies being utterly helpless and not claiming to be worthy of special treatment from God. In humility the childlike are grateful for His saving grace, receiving it inconspicuously. A child is small and unimposing in the world; in the same way we should view ourselves as insignificant before God and disregard our ego and the worries of this life in order to admire and uphold Him in complete sincerity, with no hidden motives, frankness, and simple-heartedness.

Jesus exhorts our faith to be childlike: "Assuredly, I say to you, whoever does not receive the kingdom of God as a little child will by no means enter it" (Mark 10:15). Our faith, like children, must be easily persuaded by the truth, not doubting, but receptive and trusting. Just as children grow, we too should be increasing in faith, accepting correction without questioning it, and becoming innocent and naïve regarding sinning and evil. God gives us many gifts, including entry into the kingdom of heaven, talents, peace, personality traits, and spiritual gifts. In the same way, children receive gifts, and without evaluating their value and use, they receive them gladly without wishing they were different in any way. We should also receive God's free gift in this manner, not as if we deserved it but with loving gratitude.

Pride, the opposite of humbleness, is repeatedly condemned and admonished against in the Bible. We are told it leads to divine punishment, destruction, poverty, and rebuke and that no proud person will be saved unless he or she repents (Mal. 4:1). Many scholars view it as the basis of all sin, because pride says, "I'm better than God, and I know what's right; so I will do what I want." It leads to every type of sin because it is the essence of disobedience to God's Word.

The haughtiness of Judah and Jerusalem led God to destroy them and hand them over to evil in Jeremiah 13:9–10: "Thus says the LORD: 'In this manner I will ruin the pride of Judah and the great pride of Jerusalem. This evil people, who refuse to hear My words, who follow the dictates of their hearts, and walk after other gods to serve them and worship them, shall be just like this sash which is profitable for nothing.'" The residents of Judah and Jerusalem were full of arrogance, vainglory, and boastfulness. They were too proud to listen to God and obey His commandments. The result was that God abandoned them and began working against them. This excerpt from Jeremiah is a warning to followers of Christ today; if we let pride creep in, God will work against us in order for us to repent and realize our need for Him. Of course, there is always the danger of becoming so blinded by our contemptuousness that we cannot see it and hence end up never asking for forgiveness.

One trap the devil sets is to fall into pride because of such a holy and pure life we are leading and because we have a close relationship with God. If you see yourself seeking God more than others around you and receiving more gifts and more grace, spiritual pride can very easily and subtly sneak in. This is especially cunning and therefore very difficult to detect. It is a snare in place for someone who is on the right path and who thinks they will not fall off it. Paul also acknowledges the danger of spiritual pride in 1 Corinthians 10:12 when he warns, "Therefore let him who thinks he stands take heed lest he fall." If you think you are standing strong, be careful not to fall. Paul also warns, "And don't think you know it all!" (Rom. 12:16, NLT).

In order to avoid disdainfulness, we ought to take Jesus' advice in Luke 17:10: "So likewise you, when you have done all those things which you are commanded, say, 'We are unprofitable servants. We have done what was our duty to do.'" We need to be actively seeking humility every day to avoid this lure. We should daily place ourselves before God with a humble heart, recognizing His magnitude and giving Him glory for His majesty. A way to avoid pride in general is regular and daily reading of His Word. Deuteronomy 17:18–20 instructs the king of Israel to read and follow God's Law every day of his life to keep him from becoming haughty.

Mary was one Bible character who, at a moment when most of us would have become puffed up with pride, humbled herself. The mother of Jesus, after receiving news of her honorable position in the life of the world's

God and Savior and on hearing Elizabeth's blessing, said, "How my spirit rejoices in God my Savior! For he took notice of his lowly servant girl, and from now on all generations will call me blessed" (Luke 1:47–48, NLT). Someone profoundly blessed and recognized by God called herself a "lowly servant girl"! Instead of using this privileged position to feel lofty, she uses the situation to lower herself before God and focus on His greatness and justice. This wisdom is probably one of the reasons God chose her to be Jesus' earthly mother.

Chapter 6

PURITY

No one who lives in him keeps on sinning.

1 John 3:6, niv

W E ARE MADE pure through the cleansing the blood of Jesus brings to our hearts and bodies (Heb. 10:2, 21–22). While this is working through us as we live out our lives, we are also called to purify ourselves. Paul wrote to Timothy, "Keep yourself pure" (1 Tim. 5:22, niv).

Living a life of incorruptibility is the result of loving God and having faith in Him, and it therefore leads to instant obedience to Him (1 Tim. 1:5). Obedience to Him means living out our lives according to what is written in His Word. And His Word gives many indications of what a pure life is in practice, as well as many instructions we need to observe. A common thought pattern in some churches is that because of our freedom in Christ, we do not have any guidelines or rules to follow regarding everyday living. Of course we are made righteous through faith, but to help us along the path of righteousness, there are many admonitions within the New Testament that seem to have gotten lost in today's sometimes corrupted gospel message. We need to be careful of the pendulum swinging so far away from legalism that we abuse the freedom we have been unreservedly given and displease God by our lawlessness.

For example, His Word clearly instructs us to abstain from eating blood and the meat from strangled animals (Acts 21:25). And it also directs Christians, "Don't participate in the darkness of wild parties and drunkenness, or in sexual promiscuity and immoral living, or in quarreling and jealousy" (Rom. 13:13, NLT). So we must stay away from these types of foods and the sorts of parties where drunkenness and immorality abound—where alcohol abuse, useless chatter, dirty games and jokes, and sexual looseness are rampant, even if we intend not to join in. This is because we must "avoid every kind of evil" (1 Thess. 5:22, NIV). We are called to be pure in everything, so even the places we visit should not be full of impurity.

Very occasionally it is possible for God to call us to go to be light and witnesses in such places, but we should only go when we are sure we have received specific direction from God. Satan is manifest in many different ways at these functions, and many Christians are very vulnerable to letting down their barriers and becoming desensitized and seduced by such behavior. The verse that follows offers the alternative way Christians should spend their time: "Instead, clothe yourself with the presence of the Lord Jesus Christ. And don't let yourself think about ways to indulge your evil desires" (Rom. 13:14, NLT). We are to exhibit externally the changes that have occurred within us, practicing righteous living through the presence of Jesus in our lives. Instead of going to worldly nightclubs and parties, it is better to stay at home to pray and seek the Lord.

Purity and right living in human relationships are New Testament commands that need to be adhered to as we work out our salvation. Paul basically calls us to submit to one another "in the fear of God" (Eph. 5:21, KJV). This means that the Lord is always to be the center of all our horizontal relationships, as the model of our standard of love and treatment of others. Living in love and harmony is the bottom line regarding all biblical earthly relationships (1 Pet. 3:8).

As a part of upholding this command, Paul reminds the husbands in the church to love their wives as much as they love their own bodies (Eph. 5:28). Just as Christ sacrificially gave Himself up for His bride, the church, so the husband should sacrifice himself, if necessary, for the well-being of his wife (Eph. 5:25). God does not take pleasure in those who superficially love their wives, but as Adam said out of tender love for his spouse, "This is now bone of my bones and flesh of my flesh" (Gen. 2:23). Woman was made from man's rib, symbolizing her place at his side. She was not taken from his head to control him, nor was she taken from his foot to be trodden on and used by him. God requires the husband to show love and affection to his wife. Romance between the two is important to God, so much so that under the old covenant He commanded them to have a year-long honeymoon, where the husband would dedicate one year to bringing happiness to his wife (Deut. 24:5)! Proverbs 5:18–19 also encourages the husband to enjoy sexual love toward his wife.

Wives are also to love their husbands (Titus 2:4) as well as be obedient and submissive to them (1 Pet. 3:1–2). Couples in marriages where wives put submission to God as the most important aspect and surrender to their spouses in second place have happier lifestyles than those in which the wives do not succumb to their husbands. This is partly because in a marriage, the husband and wife will always have some differences and often if the woman does not give in during a disagreement, hostility prevails. It is wiser to lay down one's arms and bite one's lip than have a tense relationship.

Regarding pure attitudes in the workplace, Paul gives advice on how we should behave in front of our bosses and how, as bosses, we should treat those under us. In the first century, more common than bosses and employees were slaves and masters, but the equivalent working relationship can still be applied today. Read the following verses substituting "slaves" with "employees" or "workers," and use "bosses" instead of "masters":

> Slaves, obey your earthly masters with respect and fear, and with sincerity of heart, just as you would obey Christ. Obey them not only to win their favor when their eye is on you, but like slaves of Christ, doing the will of God from your heart. Serve wholeheartedly, as if you were serving the Lord, not men, because you know that the Lord will reward everyone for whatever good he does, whether he is slave or free.
>
> —Ephesians 6:5–8, NIV

Paul calls for complete integrity at work, being honest and hardworking in every area, whether one's manager is looking or not.

His command for the bosses is, "And you, masters, do the same things to them, giving up threatening, knowing that your own Master also is in heaven, and there is no partiality with Him" (Eph. 6:9).

Paul also has instruction from the Old Testament for everyone with parents: "'Honor your father and mother,' which is the first commandment with promise: 'that it may be well with you and you may live long on the earth'" (Eph. 6:2–3). In an unusual twist, Paul urges parents to not act unreasonably toward their children: "Fathers, do not exasperate your children; instead, bring them up in the training and instruction of the Lord" (Eph. 6:4, NIV). While it may seem an obvious appeal to advise Christian parents to teach their children what they themselves believe, it is something that can often be overlooked. We need to be diligent in instructing our children to walk in the ways of the Lord and in teaching them to fear God. It is not something that necessarily happens automatically by attending church every Sunday; it needs to be purposely discussed as a family and dealt with throughout every step of life.

David is one example of a parent who seemed to ignore the call to instruct his children in the ways of the Lord, and the results were damaging. While he loved and feared God and walked more or less steadily before him, David's children were of a different story. His son Amnon raped his own sister, Tamar. There is no record that David corrected or punished Amnon, although he was "furious" (2 Sam. 13:21, NIV). Under the Law, Amnon should have been punished (Lev. 20:17), which could have diverted the vengeful rebellion that followed. Absalom murdered Amnon, then went into hiding. The next time Absalom appeared before his father, he received a kiss (2 Sam. 14:33), symbolizing his pardon and acceptance in the kingdom. It seems that David did not instruct his son to repent, nor did he discipline him. In fact, the next event in the Bible, recorded in 2 Samuel 15, is the start of Absalom's revolt against his father. Could this have been avoided if David had disciplined Amnon and Absalom?

First Kings 1:6 is even more blatant in proving David's indifference to correcting his sons. Of Adonijah, we are told, "His father had never interfered with him by asking, "Why do you behave as you do?" (NIV). Adonijah is another son who led a revolt against his father, David. Of course, all this rebellion was the fulfillment of the prophecy of Nathan in 2 Samuel 12:10–12, but had David disciplined his sons as God commands us to, maybe the punishment of his sin with Bathsheba would have come in a different form and not from within his own household.

Noah's son, Ham, dishonored his father by seeing him naked and telling his brothers about Noah's disgrace (Gen. 9:22). He and his descendants were therefore cursed (Gen. 9:25).

Some people say if their children would honor them, then they wouldn't aggravate them; or if their wives were more submissive, then they would love them as Christ loves the church, and vice-versa. However, these attitudes are unbiblical. No matter how our spouse, parents, or children treat us, we must still obey God and follow His teaching regarding these relationships. (In some abusive situations, it may be best to remove yourself and seek help.)

While we should observe these rules, we also need to be aware of inventing our own commandments that are not part of God's Word. From reading the book of Colossians, we can tell that many heresies and false teachings had already permeated the church in Colossae. Paul touches on the surface of the church's dogma and corrects it throughout the book.

One of the untruths they held to was legalism in the form of consuming certain foods, circumcision, and religious festival days. Nowadays, these specific regulations are unusual, although this type of rule invention occurs in other external laws, such as forbidding working on the Sabbath (which is actually a Saturday, not Sunday), requiring the use of specific clothes, banning make-up, placing restrictions on women in the ministry, rules regarding the frequency of Holy Communion, the prohibition of television watching, and so forth. While such policies may seem spiritual, they actually move the focus from God and holy living to the regulation itself, thereby annulling Christ's atoning sacrifice on the cross. We need to be on guard against the pool of thought that salvation is ours through the union of faith in Christ with human theorem adapted from the Bible.

However, always bear in mind that it can be useless to argue over a small area of a Christian's lifestyle if it is not hurting anyone or putting anyone in danger of losing his or her salvation. Sometimes it is best to put small differences aside and concentrate on loving one another. If we have misunderstood a small part of doctrine, God may not always correct His people; but if we are in danger of losing our life, He does. Our goal should be to seek biblical backup for everything we do and everything we hear preached. There are many wolves out there who will try and trick us any way they can to take us off the path of salvation.

BREAD AND WINE

> Then Jesus said to them, "Most assuredly, I say to you, unless you eat the flesh of the Son of Man and drink His blood, you have no life in you. Whoever eats My flesh and drinks My blood has eternal life, and I will raise him up at the last day. For My flesh is food indeed, and My blood is drink indeed."
>
> —JOHN 6:53–55

Just before Jesus gave up His body on the cross for the forgiveness of sins, He left us instructions that must not be forgotten or ignored. We are to eat bread and drink wine while with thanksgiving we remember, celebrate, and announce His death (1 Cor. 11:26).

The bread represents Jesus' body, which was sacrificed for us. As we eat it in memory of Him, we are physically and spiritually declaring His death in our own life. His death lives in us and leads us to the path of life, so we can live in freedom from the slavery of sin and death. His sacrifice is now a part of our life, and we celebrate it with joy rather than sorrow.

The wine represents Jesus' blood poured out for us, symbolizing the new covenant between God and His people. Jeremiah summed this up in a nutshell when he prophesied, "I will put My law in their minds, and write it on their hearts; and I will be their God, and they shall be My people" (Jer. 31:33). Jesus fulfilled all the regulations that we would have needed to follow under the Mosaic Law, and we are now made right before God through faith in Him.

As we take the bread and wine, we are commemorating our freedom from the bondage of sin through Jesus' body and blood, given up for us. We are also proclaiming the blessings that come with the new relationship man has with God through Jesus' atoning work, such as forgiveness, peace, love, hope, mercy, joy, righteousness, grace, godly wisdom, holiness, and eternal life.

As this is a sacred act, not to be taken lightly or with a reckless, thoughtless attitude, we are to inspect our temperament before taking the bread and wine, scrutinizing our life to see if there are any hidden faults or sins within us that we need to renounce. In Paul's words, "A man ought to examine himself before he eats of the bread and drinks of the cup" (1 Cor. 11:28, NIV); therefore, we must search within ourselves to find any ungodly attitudes lurking or any dishonesty we have displayed in our actions or speech. If we find any such wrongdoing within, we must confess it to God and ask for forgiveness and for help to overcome it. Before taking the Lord's Supper, as part of our act of worship, we also need to thank and praise Jesus for His body and blood.

Anyone who takes the bread and wine willy-nilly without real faith is not saved. In fact, Paul reveals in 1 Corinthians 11:27 that "whoever eats this bread or drinks this cup of the Lord in an unworthy manner will be guilty of the body and blood of the Lord." He even mentions that "anyone who eats and drinks without recognizing the body of the Lord eats and drinks judgment on himself" (v. 29, NIV). It is a serious thing to disrespect the living God. For this reason each person should take time to analyze his life and humble himself before breaking the bread.

It is critical to note that the verse quoted above from John 6 must never be taken out of context. In order to understand it fully, it is of utmost importance that it is used with the whole of Jesus' speech, from John 6:27–65. Sometimes this verse is used and abused as an excuse to live a lazy, flesh-pleasing life. Some people have interpreted it as the only requirement to be saved. Within its context, Jesus clearly remarks that faith is indispensable with taking communion in verse 35 and that we need to be living in Him and spiritually feeding on Him (v. 57). Part of the symbolic act of taking the bread and wine is fulfilling the significance behind it. We should be regularly coming to Jesus to eat His flesh, which is the bread of heaven, giving us real nourishment. This is part of living a life in accordance with Jesus' words, feeding off who He is and what the Scriptures tell us about Him, following Him at every turn and opportunity down the pathway of life.

The breaking of bread is meant to be done together with the whole church to represent the unity of the body of Christ (1 Cor. 10:17), just as Jesus carried out the first breaking of bread in the context of an intimate meal with fellow believers.

HATRED OF SIN

I will set before my eyes no vile thing. The deeds of faithless men I hate; they will not cling to me. Men of perverse heart shall be far from me; I will have nothing to do with evil. Whoever slanders his neighbor in secret, him will I put to silence; whoever has haughty eyes and a proud heart, him will I not endure. My eyes will be on the faithful in the land, that they may dwell with me; he whose walk is blameless will minister to me. No one who practices deceit will dwell in my house; no one who speaks falsely will stand in my presence. Every morning I will put to silence all the wicked in the land; I will cut off every evildoer from the city of the LORD.

—PSALM 101:3–8, NIV

Psalm 101 is David's description of his hatred of iniquity and his commitment to reign righteously. His abhorrence of evil leads him to:

- forbid his eyes to rest upon anything unclean (v. 3);
- loathe immorality (v. 3);
- disallow unbelievers' deeds to stay in his mind (v. 3);
- not associate with rebellious people (v. 4);
- correct evildoing constantly (v. 8), and silence whoever criticizes others (v. 5);

- be intolerable of the proud (v. 5) and liars (v. 7);
- flee from sinfulness (v. 8);
- dwell with the godly and faithful (v. 6); and
- lead a blameless life (v. 7).

In verse 7, David explains he is even careful of who his associates are and that he does not allow anyone dubious into his administration. When the righteousness of God is alive in us, we will detest wickedness to the same degree David demonstrates in this psalm. Hating ungodliness is being grieved by evildoing, just as Paul was in Athens when he observed the idol-worshiping (Acts 17:16). A commitment to hating corruption brings out virtuous and blameless living before God. It causes us to experience righteous anger from within at injustice and to feel saddened by the iniquity we see around us.

Such disgust and separation from transgressions is necessary to live in fellowship with God. Sin is alien to His perfect nature, and it is disobedience to His divine will. We are made in the image of God, and so are called to reflect His holiness in all we do. The first sin in the Bible, committed by Adam and Eve, has become the hallmark of sin, which is disobedience against God's Word. Before any sin was committed, they were able to walk around naked and free from shame in God's and each other's presences. They were completely innocent. As soon as they ate the fruit, they felt embarrassment at their nakedness, and so, covered themselves up. The feeble covering with the fig leaves symbolizes their separation from God, as they were no longer morally innocent. This shows how repugnant sin is to God. It is not even allowed in His presence. God then sacrificed an animal to cover their disgrace. Blood needed to be shed, just as Jesus has become the perfect sacrifice for us and we are now allowed in God's presence again. In the same way that God separated Adam and Eve from His presence by the garments of animal skin, we need to separate ourselves from lawlessness.

A fruit of the abhorrence of sin is the feeling of repugnance and offense when we hear about unrighteous practices and attitudes. It is even manifest when we detest watching scenes where perversity is practiced, and we dislike even listening about what the ungodly do in their spare time. When we do expose ourselves to hearing or seeing sinful acts, we feel a temporary separation from God's peace until we ask for forgiveness and seek Him again. If we are exposed to this material by accident, we will perceive this temporary distance from God, but as soon as it is out of our mind, we feel God's warm presence and love again.

The result of this sort of attitude is hungering and thirsting for righteousness (Matt. 5:6) and clinging to what is good (Rom. 12:9). When we momentarily slip and commit a sin, whether it be gossip, a lustful thought, or criticism of others, as soon as we realize the mistake, because of our sheer disgust of disobedience to God, we feel disappointment and anger with ourselves; therefore, we repent and ask for God's forgiveness, as taught in the Lord's Prayer.

In Romans 6:12–13, we are told to "not let sin control the way you live; do not give in to sinful desires. Do not let any part of your body become an instrument of evil to serve sin. Instead, give yourselves completely to God, for you were dead, but now you have new life" (NLT). Paul's formula to combat, flee from, and therefore hate unrighteousness is remembering that we are dead to transgressions (Rom. 6:6–7) and alive in God (v. 8). We must battle against and repudiate the reign of ungodliness in our lives (v. 12), consequently focusing on giving ourselves completely to God and celebrating this new life He has freely given us by His grace. The result of this will be freedom from the power of sin and separation from its practices.

When people around us are having a discussion and what they are saying is displeasing to God—for example, it may contain judgments, criticisms, hatred, unjustified anger, or sinful things—as the light of the world we must not take part in such conversations and, if necessary, stick up for what is right. If asked our opinion, we need to speak God's truth, stand out, and be different, even if it means suffering the consequences. All Christians should stand up for justice and flee from unrighteousness.

At this point we must never forget to hate the sin but love the sinner, and never judge anyone for the wickedness they do but be full of unfailing love toward everyone. As in 1 Corinthians 16:14, we must "do everything with love" (NLT).

God has many wonderful promises for those who hate sin and break themselves away from its power: protection and delivery from evil (Ps. 97:10), understanding (Ps. 119:104), love for God's law (Ps. 119:163), and honor and joy (Ps. 45:7), amongst many others. But the most wonderful reward for those who separate and purify themselves for God is to be able to meet Him face to face and spend eternity with Him.

RESISTING TEMPTATION

> Be self-controlled and alert. Your enemy the devil prowls around like a roaring lion looking for someone to devour. Resist him, standing firm in the faith, because you know that your brothers throughout the world are undergoing the same kind of sufferings.
> —1 PETER 5:8–9, NIV

Our strong enemy (Ps. 18:17) is a very real and serious threat to our souls. He will do anything to make us fall down and sin against God. He is very angry because he knows he will ultimately lose the battle he has been fighting against God. As Revelation 12:12 states, "He is filled with fury, because he knows that his time is short" (NIV). Therefore, he desires more than anything to see Christians fall and will go to any length to steal our salvation, destroy, and kill us.

Jesus reveals that of Peter, Satan "has asked to sift you as wheat. But I have prayed for you, Simon, that your faith may not fail" (Luke 22:31–32, NIV). The footnotes in the New International Version explain that the first *you* here in the original Greek is plural. We should fight off our temptations to sin by the grace of God without giving up until we overcome them, especially knowing that Satan wants to kill us and take our salvation away from us; one way he starts this process is to win us over to our own desires and weaknesses by tempting us. Those who do not give in to temptation are promised that their name will not be erased from the Lamb's Book of Life: "He who overcomes shall be clothed in white garments, and I will not blot out his name from the Book of Life; but I will confess his name before My Father and before His angels" (Rev. 3:5).

The reason why falling into temptation is so serious is because ultimately giving in to it could lead to our access being denied into the kingdom of God. Jesus demonstrates this in the parable of the banquet (Luke 14:16–24), which deals with guests who had been invited to the feast of the kingdom of heaven. God's original plan was to invite His people to spend eternity with Him, but one after the other, they came up with poor excuses as to why they couldn't attend. The excuse of two of the men was that they had just made a business investment and were too busy. The third man's excuse was that he had just gotten married and was otherwise occupied. Therefore, the poor, the crippled, the blind, and the lame were invited. This group represents the Gentiles who now have access to God's kingdom basically because the original guests gave in to the temptations that this world offers, so they could not enter themselves.

However, this parable also serves as a warning to us even today. It is possible for us to also miss going to heaven for the same reasons that some of the original Jews did—we get distracted by even the simple, seemingly harmless temptations of life that are not essentially sins, such as when our families, our children, our spouses, our jobs, hobbies, or business ventures, for example, become more important than hearing God's Word and obeying it. This is where many Christians fall down. When sins are obviously sins, it is sometimes easier to avoid them. But when we sin against God with something that on its own is not a sin but has been made into a sin because it has taken the number one spot in our lives, which belongs to God, then it is harder to see and easier to do.

Sometimes as this happens, we can get into a comfortable routine in life and conveniently "forget" God through the fast pace of this postmodern society. Or we just put Him to the side, and whenever we have a spare ten minutes or so, then we'll pray and read the Bible. It is so easy to get caught up with mundane tasks, such as going to work, doing the housework, going to the gym, doing things for the children, and commitments at church. Focusing first on these things does not allow us to live a life hungering for God, completely dedicated to Him in everything and always growing in the faith.

If this is a reflection of your life, where God has been tucked to the side or just left to church services and half-hearted prayers in which you are not pouring yourself out before Him, you need to repent and renew your covenant with Him. Our calling is to "submit yourselves, then, to God" (James 4:7, NIV), indicating that we should be seeking God with all our heart every day of the year. We should be completely subject to Him in all our decisions and actions. When we live a life like this, James continues by saying, only then will the devil "flee from you" when we resist him (James 4:7, NIV). But if we are not totally submissive to God, then we won't have power to resist the devil; and he therefore will not flee from us.

Some common temptations that can take us off the heavenward path when given in to are: the cares and pleasures of this world (Luke 8:14), the desire to be rich (1 Tim. 6.9), riches themselves (Matt. 19:21–22), seeking prosperity (Luke 12:16–21), difficulties under persecution (Mark 4:17), argumentativeness and selfishness (James 4:1–6), anger (Eph. 4:30), envy (Ps. 73:3), greed (Matt. 16:26), pride (Philippians 2:3), the influence of evildoers (Ps. 1:1), and sexual desires and adultery (Prov. 6:25–29), amongst others.

Notice that most of these focus on the desires that come from within us, which are part of our human nature. These yearnings can be placed into three categories, which are described in 1 John 2:16 (NIV):

- "The cravings of sinful man"—This means our exaggerated material and non-material appetites, including for food, drink, sleep, sex, indulgence and luxuries, rest, business, work, studying, power, money, following a dream, building a reputation, over-the-top desires for material goods, and any addictions or extreme interests which take our focus off God. This may be a book, music, collection, habit, sport, sports team, the Internet or web sites, shopping, television, films, activities, games, objects, accessories, or a certain type of entertainment or hobby. Many of these elements are not necessarily sins on their own; but rather, anything done obsessively, including watching Christian films, for example, becomes fleshy and carnal. But we are called to live in the spirit and focus on spiritual things (2 Cor. 4:18).

- "The lust of his [man's] eyes"—This category involves the appeal to take our lives in our own hands and do what we think is best from our own point of view. This is essentially not entrusting our lives to God's hands.
- "And the boasting of what he [man] has and does"—This is to say, self-importance, self-esteem, self-infatuation, self-exaltation, and basically living to please oneself, not God.

As Christians, these distractions need to be tamed and controlled in our minds as we come under submission to God and strive to lead a life of holiness as we are being sanctified by the Holy Spirit. Jesus prepares us for such evils and sums them up neatly in Luke 21:34–36:

> Be careful, or your hearts will be weighed down with dissipation, drunkenness and the anxieties of life, and that day will close on you unexpectedly like a trap. For it will come upon all those who live on the face of the whole earth. Be always on the watch, and pray that you may be able to escape all that is about to happen, and that you may be able to stand before the Son of Man. (NIV)

Our enemy actively searches for opportunities to tempt us into sinning and to accuse us before God. He seeks footholds into our soul (Eph. 4:25–27, NLT), which open up when we sin, giving him the right to cause grief and greater evil in our lives. Sinning often has a ripple effect that can affect us in seemingly unrelated ways, sometimes possibly even later in life.

This happened to Reuben, the son of Jacob. In Genesis 35:22, we learn that he sinned against God and his father by sleeping with his father's concubine, Bilhah. Many years later, as Jacob was on his deathbed, Reuben reaped what he had sown. Jacob prophesied, "You will no longer excel, for you went up onto your father's bed, onto my couch and defiled it" (Gen. 49:4, NIV). He did not escape punishment, and his sin allowed the devil to gain an opening into his life and curse him.

Ephesians 4:25–27 (NLT) also shows that our sins, especially when we sin against other people, allow evil an opening to our souls, causing us difficulties and strife. This is all the more reason why we need to stand guard and be aware of the schemes of the devil.

The way to guard our souls is to be born of God and therefore not continue to sin. When we are there, the devil is prohibited from harming us, as it says in 1 John 5:18: "We know that anyone born of God does not continue to sin; the one who was born of God keeps him safe, and the evil one cannot harm him" (NIV). If we want protection from temptation and problems, we need to defend ourselves against sin and apathy toward God. Romans 12:20–21 tells us that we should overcome evil with good by treating our human enemies well. This is the essence of winning spiritual battles.

Thank God that by His love and mercy, the Bible contains different techniques and thought patterns to focus on to guide us and equip us against falling down before corruption.

Before Jesus started His ministry, He was led by the Spirit into the desert to be tempted by the devil. It was a stage He was obliged to pass through before becoming a well-known preacher and miracle worker. The main feature that accompanied His forty-day period of temptation was fasting, teaching us that fasting is a powerful weapon when faced with evil enticements. (See the section entitled "Fasting" in Chapter 13.)

The Book of Hebrews contains practical hints on how to stand against the devil, such as encouraging others, who in turn will encourage us. In Hebrews 3:13, we are advised, "But exhort one another daily, while it is called 'Today,' lest any of you be hardened through the deceitfulness of sin." We are exhorted to live in constant communion and fellowship with other believers, sharing our thoughts, experiences, struggles, love, and giftings. This is an approach that helps in standing firm and not giving in to evil. The writer of Hebrews explains the urgency of acting on today's struggle rather than leaving it for tomorrow, because he recognizes that while we allow our old, sinful self to fester, the time we can experience God's grace and renewal may run out. Therefore, we need to act with seriousness to put off our old sinful self with our evil temptations to walk in the light of God.

A shock tactic is also used at the beginning of Hebrews 2 to awaken the Christians who are tempted to sin and turn back to their old life. The author reminds them that those who do not pay attention to God, live in obedience to Him, and accept salvation in Jesus Christ are justly punished: "Therefore we must give the more earnest heed to the things we have heard, lest we drift away. For if the word spoken through angels proved stead-fast, and every transgression and disobedience received a just reward, how shall we escape if we neglect so great a salvation?" (Heb. 1:1–2). The essayist encourages us to focus on the message and truth of the gospel, because those who do not will not inherit eternal life. He then goes on to point out the authenticity of the gospel in verse 4.

Paul understood how great the threat of the devil is to us. He likened Christians to fully armed soldiers in the battle against evil:

- "Put on the whole armor of God, that you may be able to stand against the wiles of the devil" (Eph. 6:11).
- "Stand therefore, having girded your waist with truth" (Heb. 6:14). He recognizes the importance of truth in spiritual warfare, so he illustrates it fixed around our middle as a belt. *Truth* refers to the Word of God and the person of Jesus. The belly symbolizes greed in the Bible, so the fact that truth is to be figuratively strapped around our waist means that the person of Jesus within us, Bible studying, and biblical knowl-edge combat, purify, and nullify our own sinful desires and greed. They give us strength to defend ourselves from the devil's schemes.
- "Having put on the breastplate of righteousness" (Heb. 6:14). Our righteousness and purity in Jesus Christ must blaze before us, protecting the heart in the same way a breastplate would. This is because when we behave righteously, we have no footholds left open for the devil to attack our heart. It is the protection over the entrance of our soul. This also symbolizes that character wins conflicts, not vain words or violence.
- "Shod your feet with the preparation of the gospel of peace" (Heb. 6:15). Our feet are significant because it is with our feet that we gain momentum to run and walk. In all we do,

in all our movements, actions, and wherever we go, we must always be prepared to share the message of the gospel, which brings peace to those who receive it gladly. "The preparation of the gospel of peace" is to be fitted on the soldier's feet like a shoe and symbolizes protection for wherever we tread, meaning that spreading the gospel of Jesus Christ will guide and safeguard us wherever we go.

- "Taking the shield of faith" (Heb. 6:16). The shield represents steadfastness in our faith in God. We are to use the certainty faith brings us to stand firmly against accusations and lies from the devil. Shields in the Bible figuratively represent God's protection (Gen. 15:1) and His faithfulness (Ps. 91:4), which both strengthen us in battle.

- "Take the helmet of salvation" (Heb. 6:17). Helmets, as a protective covering for the head and brain, demonstrate our security and assurance of salvation. They are indispensable during warfare. They also signify the perfect mental health God gives only to those who are saved.

- "Sword of the Spirit, which is the word of God" (Heb. 6:17). The sword of the Spirit is the only piece of the armor used for attack, suggesting the use of Biblical knowledge and understanding to correct any false statements launched at us by the powers of darkness. The sheer spiritual power the Word of God possesses can cut down any strongholds during combat. Jesus' own tactic was to fire Scripture at the devil when temptations arose in Matthew 4:3–11. The analogy of the sword of the Spirit as God's word is explained in Hebrews 4:12: "For the word of God is living and active. Sharper than any double-edged sword, it penetrates even to dividing soul and spirit, joints and marrow; it judges the thoughts and attitudes of the heart" (NIV).

- "Praying always with all prayer and supplication in the Spirit" (Heb. 6:18). This reminds us that it is with God's help and force that we will win the battle (1 Sam. 17:47), so we must always rely on Him in constant prayer. It is through prayer and walking with the Lord that we get closer to Him, which in turn strengthens us against temptation, as the psalmist experienced in Psalm 94:18: "When I said, 'My foot is slipping,' your love, O LORD, supported me" (NIV).

- "Being watchful to this end with all perseverance and supplication for all the saints" (Heb. 6:18). (See the section entitled "Watchfulness" in Chapter 12.)

Notice that the armor of God does not include any protection for the back of the soldier because fleeing is not an option!

Over and over again we are advised to pray against falling into temptation in the Bible. Jesus stressed the importance of asking for God's help in protection against succumbing to temptation. In Luke's Gospel He refers to it three times—in the Lord's Prayer and twice in Luke 22, speaking to His disciples. It needs to be a part of our daily prayers, because falling into temptation is a life-threatening reality. The devil can spring on us at any time, God permitting, so we always need to be covered in prayer and ready. We ought to look to God and rely on His help to overcome temptation instead of waiting on our own strength. We need to trust Him, because "God is faithful; he will not let you be tempted beyond what you can bear. But when you are tempted, he will also provide a way out so that you can stand up under it" (1 Cor. 10:13, NIV).

Another enticement believers face is the one to actually give up the Christian race. In order to combat this, the Book of Hebrews tries to motivate its readers to focus on Jesus' sacrifice and victory. Its inspirational speech goes like this:

Therefore we also, since we are surrounded by so great a cloud of witnesses, let us lay aside every weight, and the sin which so easily ensnares us, and let us run with endurance the race that is set before us, looking unto Jesus, the author and finisher of our faith, who for the joy that was set before Him endured the cross, despising the shame, and has sat down at the right hand of the throne of God. For consider Him who endured such hostility from sinners against Himself, lest you become weary and discouraged in your souls.

—HEBREWS 12:1–3

Anyone who needs a thrust will surely feel spurred on after that! The writer prompts us to take encouragement from all the examples of endurance and victorious lives previously mentioned in Hebrews 11, such as those of Abraham, Joseph, and Moses. With their example in mind, we must resist sin and as an athlete, run at a steady pace the race of life. Energetic imagery is used to stimulate us to give our everything to the task set before us. We must concentrate on Jesus, who endured torture and humiliation in order to receive His eternal reward, His place of honor at the right hand of God. Therefore we should also remember our recompense so as to enable us to run firmly and not slip.

FLEEING FROM LUSTFULNESS

You have heard that it was said to those of old, 'You shall not commit adultery.' But I say to you that whoever looks at a woman to lust for her has already committed adultery with her in his heart.

—MATTHEW 5:27–28

Jesus unveils that we must lead a pure thought life, because adultery is not just a physical act; it can take place inside us, too. Merely thinking sexual thoughts toward someone we are not married to is a sin before God.

Nowadays, a big temptation related to this can be magazines, newspapers, the Internet, television, and film. These media contain many sexually-provocative images to incite our interest and draw our attention. As a people redeemed by Christ's blood, we should avert our minds and stop looking when sexual stimuli and pictures appear before us. We need to keep our desires constantly in check and ask ourselves, Are we watching something that provokes lustfulness? Are we committing adultery? There can be a very fine line between admiring someone's beauty and accommodating lustful thoughts.

> Your eye is a lamp that provides light for your body. When your eye is good, your whole body is filled with light. But when your eye is bad, your whole body is filled with darkness. And if the light you think you have is actually darkness, how deep that darkness is!
>
> —MATTHEW 6:22–23, NLT

Jesus instructs us to be vigilant where we put our eyes. Even walking down the street, there can be sexually provocative advertising on billboards and posters. It can also be found in respectable newspapers and even in television programs and films supposedly suitable for children. In a world where advertising in particular aims to touch our senses, especially our sense of vision, which is the most influential, we have to be wary wherever we are because it is so easy for lustful thoughts to slip in unnoticed. Remember, it does not have to be what the world considers pornographic to whip up lustful thoughts. It is good practice to get into the habit of turning away when someone seductively dressed or when a seducing advertisement is before us. The beach is also a place to watch where our eyes and thoughts wander.

In Genesis 39, Joseph demonstrates just this. Every day he was before Pharaoh's seducing wife with all her riches and Egyptian beauty. "She kept putting pressure on Joseph day after day, but he refused to sleep with her, and he kept out of her way as much as possible" (Gen. 39:10, NLT). He stubbornly resisted, saying, "How could I do such a wicked thing? It would be a great sin against God" (v. 9, NLT). Faced with the opportunity to commit adultery, Joseph focused his thoughts on the Lord and the magnitude of the wickedness involved in sleeping with someone else's wife. He revealed real wisdom by avoiding his master's spouse at all costs, even fleeing from her (Gen. 39:12).

In a world where sex before marriage is expected—and often with more than one partner—we must stand as firm like Joseph and "run from sexual sin" (1 Cor. 6:18, NLT) to maintain the sanctity of marriage.

Sex, created by God, was only intended to take place within the safe walls of a marital relationship (Acts 15:28, KJV), because the only stable place to raise children is in a loving relationship between a man and a woman. A whole book in the Bible deals with the beauty of sexual, passionate love, the Song of Solomon. One warning that is issued again and again in the book is not to awaken love until the right time (Song of Sol. 2:7; 3:5; 8:4).

Many teenage magazines discuss sex in great details, encouraging young people barely going through puberty to sexually experiment way before they are physically or emotionally ready, abusing the true identity God gave sexual love. Because of this, for many people, sexual love, or *eros*, has lost its original beauty God bestowed upon it. They don't understand the real significance of sexual intercourse, and instead it is unnaturally induced with obscene images, toys, and false love, which are all artificial distractions, deceiving people about the real essence of intimate love between a man and a woman.

First Corinthians 6:15–17 explains that those who have more than one sexual partner outside marriage leave a piece of themselves with every person they sleep with. This disrespect toward one's own body (1 Cor. 6:18) leads to emotional and relational problems. This unnatural arousal of sexual desire before its proper time has lead to frustration, brokenness, problematic relationships, and a defective society full of psychological problems. Christians are commanded to control their lusts and bodies (1 Thess. 4:3–5) because their calling is one of purity. A Christian who does sin in this area will be punished by God (1 Thess. 4:6–7).

The way to restrain unhealthy sexual desires starts in our intellect (Mark 7:21). When we feel sinful sexual urges arousing, we must be cautious not to accommodate them, dwell on them, or give them any opportunity or leeway. We need to be alert to divert such thinking and immediately tell it (or rather, remind the tempter behind it) of Scripture verses such as Hebrews 3:1, which instructs us to constantly reflect on Jesus; and 1 Corinthians 6:18, "Flee from sexual immorality" (NIV).

Samson suffered tragically due to his inability to control his lust, despite the hand of God on his life. An angel declared his birth to his mother with similar wording used to proclaim the births of Isaac, John the Baptist, and Jesus. Samson was born miraculously to a previously barren mother, as were Isaac and John. Even before Samson's birth he was declared as set-apart to God (Judg. 13:5) and instructions were given to his parents as to how to bring him up. For forty years prior to Samson's birth, God had not given Israel a judge, and the Philistines were ruling over them. Israel was in drastic need of solid leadership to free them from Philistine control. Judges 13:24–25 tells us that Samson "grew, and the LORD blessed him. And the Spirit of the LORD began to move upon him." As we continue to read Judges 14 and 15, we see how the Lord was working in his life. Samson obviously had great potential as Israel's judge; a ray of hope in a despondent Israel.

However, in Chapter 16, Samson's weakness regarding sex and his desire for women is revealed when he spends half a night with a prostitute, marking the start of his downfall. From then on, things changed for him, as we never again read that the Spirit of the Lord came upon him as He previously did. Samson then falls in love with the treacherous Delilah, and with her seductive spirit she is able to subdue him, where thousands of men had gone amiss. The result was that Samson lost his sight and became a Philistine slave and entertainment trophy. What went wrong?

Unfortunately, his attraction to women and lack of self-control got the better of him. He allowed himself to be a slave to passion, and with it ignored God's commandment that marriage with a woman outside of Israel was prohibited (Deut. 7:3). Because of his lasciviousness and Delilah's sexual lure, he prostituted his vocation to a woman from the enemy camp. The result was that God left him. Had he been able to control his biological urges for women and waited for God to give him the right wife, the second part of his life would have been free of humiliation and slavery. Samson's escapades forewarn us that lustfulness leads us away from God into the hands of the enemy.

Chapter 7

CLEAN MOUTH

Let no corrupt word proceed out of your mouth, but what is good
for necessary edification, that it may impart grace to the hearers.

Ephesians 4:29

W

E MUST WATCH everything that comes out of our mouths. We are even told to steer clear of talking about worthless things of no help or importance to our spiritual life. All our conversations should be helpful to build up others.

> Avoid godless chatter, because those who indulge in it will become more and more ungodly.
>
> —2 Timothy 2:16, NIV

This *godless chatter* refers to the absence of God and holy things in our conversations. We therefore need to control our mouths to only speak what is fruitful, talking about God and spiritual things rather than the things of this world. If we do not, we will find ourselves becoming distant from God. Pointless and meaningless comments and remarks are also useless and should be averted. Banter about the latest worldly sinful films, gossip, sports stars, celebrities, and so forth are all hollow and put a wedge between us and God. We need to understand the difference between what is helpful and what we think is allowed by the law (1 Cor. 10:23).

Unclean mouths reside even among those in the ministry, as well as amongst "ordinary" members of the congregation. Sometimes those who have a Christian vocation (i.e., they have dedicated their lives to His work) act as if they are exempt from living a life with pure speech. Some of us live with an impure mouth either out of ignorance or lack of wanting to deny the flesh, or we are so used to hearing the Holy Scriptures that we switch off from them and have forgotten what they contain. It is possible to be someone who prays fervently, who nearly always has a time alone with God, who enjoys reading the Bible, has many spiritual giftings, and at the same time has a dirty mouth.

One main characteristic of such a life is unwholesome talk with endless conversations about useless facts or observations, which do not edify anyone. It doesn't seem to necessarily do any harm, either, and may be entertaining, but in fact such chatter is spiritually detrimental and can kill. Even telling indirectly impure jokes numbs us to God's high moral standards. To sum up, even though some of us are outwardly moral, we do not necessarily have a clean heart; therefore, our talk is tainted, and such impurity often easily goes unnoticed in the church. Paul rebukes such people by saying, "For the Kingdom of God is not just a lot of talk; it is living by God's power" (1 Cor. 4:20, NLT).

A common mindset we can have is one that believes that simple conversation, as long as we do not swear or lie, is harmless. The Bible paints a very different picture. In James 3:6, James calls the tongue "a fire, a world of evil among the parts of the body. It corrupts the whole person, sets the whole course of his life on fire, and is itself set on fire by hell" (NIV). In verse 8, he explains that man cannot tame the tongue. Only God can, so there is hope for us! Proverbs views many useless words as destructive. "A chattering fool comes to ruin," it says (Prov. 10:8, NIV). Therefore every time we open our mouths to speak, we should carefully measure their use (Prov. 29:20).

We should recognize that even truthful words can cause damage. Saying something hurtful and excusing it by declaring, "I'm only being honest," is as destructive as a fire. Before speaking, we must ask ourselves, Will what I'm going to say offend who I'm talking to? and, Will it be helpful to them or not? We must always be on the lookout to avoid dissensions with our neighbors and brothers. An unruly tongue can even destroy a marriage.

Judging others is also a trap many of us fall into.

> Judge not, that you be not judged. For with what judgment you judge, you will be judged; and with the measure you use, it will be measured back to you.
>
> —MATTHEW 7:1–2

No one has been given the right to evaluate anyone else on Earth. Only God has that entitlement (John 5:21). Therefore, we are in the wrong when we give a negative opinion about a person or measure their worth. This includes famous people and political figures, no matter how unholy their ethics are. Only God knows everyone's thoughts and hidden motives, so when we assess others, it is normally an incorrect judgment.

Even knocking companies and organizations is wrong. If you find fault with them, you may be unknowingly criticizing their board of directors or founders, who are people made in the image of God. When a group of friends or family members start a mass criticism of someone or a people group, it can be the easiest thing to join in and give your opinion. Sometimes we don't even realize we are making an adverse comment, especially if it was someone else who started the conversation. In situations such as this, we must bite our lips, imagine a zipper over our mouths, and close it up so as not to sadden the Holy Spirit and bring judgment upon ourselves. Jesus never spoke negatively about anything in vain, but as the Judge of the world, He used constructive criticism to point out faults.

Another type of criticizing that can be particularly hurtful and sly is the disapproval of other believers because of their faith. Paul urges us to "accept other believers who are weak in faith, and don't argue with them about what they think is right or wrong. For instance, one person believes it's all right to eat anything. But another believer with a sensitive conscience will eat only vegetables" (Rom. 14:1–2, NLT). Many, many times I have heard Christians challenge other believers as to why they are vegetarians and how if you are a Christian, it is wrong to be a vegetarian. However, Paul explains that if someone believes it is wrong to eat meat, the rest of us should just leave them to it without looking down on them. There may be a personal reason behind someone being a vegetarian, such as a vow to God or even a personal disgust at the way animals are killed. Another explanation could be a bad experience with eating meat, seeing a dying animal, or a food allergy. In fact, Paul actually advises us not to eat meat ourselves if we are in the company of a believing vegetarian who is upset by it (Rom. 14:15).

This practice can be applied to many other examples. One prominent example that has caused divisions in some Brazilian churches is the question of women wearing skirts and not cutting their hair. Many less traditional Christians and churches disagree and believe that women can wear almost any type of trousers and skirts and can cut and dye their hair as much as they like. In my experience, it is wiser to not criticize the traditionalist churches and congregations but just accept them as they are. If a woman from a freer congregation wants to visit one of these churches, it is probably more prudent to wear a skirt, so as not to scandalize a brother or sister for whom Christ died (Rom. 14:15). Of course, she should never claim to always wear a skirt and never dye or cut her hair, because that would be hypocrisy. As Paul pointed out, "You may believe there's nothing wrong with what you are doing, but keep it between yourself and God" (Rom. 14:22, NLT).

There are also some churches I know of in Brazil and England that instruct women to use a veil as a head covering, a precept taken from 1 Corinthians 11:3–16. Again, instead of arguing with them, it is wiser for a woman to cover her head while in such churches than to criticize them for doing what they believe is right.

Instead of using our mouths to pass judgment, Jesus reminds us why it is so important to speak wholesome words. He said, "But I say to you that for every idle word men may speak, they will give account of it in the Day of Judgment. For by your words you will be justified, and by your words you will be condemned" (Matt. 12:36–37). So one shouldn't talk to anyone about people's or churches' problems and mistakes, especially to nonbelievers. Instead, we should be a filter for our family and friends about what goes on in other people's lives and at church. Speaking dismissively about another

Christian, for example, may mean your family and friends will view all Christians by what you say about them. We need self-discipline in what we relate because an uncontrolled tongue is lethal. Always control your speech and, as Proverbs 20:19 insinuates, don't talk too much, because it can sometimes lead us up a sticky path we can't get off.

Gossip is a malicious vice that similarly causes discord, splitting friends and churches.

> A perverse man sows strife, And a whisperer separates the best
> of friends.
>
> —Proverbs 16:28

Gossiping is also very contagious because a gossiper can exaggerate and have a wonderful imagination. In the same way that a little yeast works through the whole batch of dough, a little small talk can work through an entire church, so we must always be on guard against it. Anyone who talks unkindly about other people's business and claims to be a Christian is not, because "nor slanderers nor swindlers will inherit the kingdom of God" (1 Cor. 6:10, NIV).

The result of Miriam and Aaron's jealous meddling regarding Moses' foreign wife and his special relationship with God was rebuke and punishment (Num. 12:1–12). As Miriam did, we will catch spiritual leprosy if we chitchat too much. This means that God will make us spiritual outcasts, as He temporarily did to Miriam. We must also steer clear of the "I was only joking" deceitful tittle-tattle (Prov. 26:18–19), which makes a fool out of people and causes dissension, whether it appears so or not.

Complaining is likewise addictive, and many of us get drawn into it. We complain about our situations, circumstances, hardships, our families, spouses, injustices, churches, the traffic, the weather, the news, television, strangers, society, our jobs, and the list goes on. It can also be so easy and very pleasing to the flesh to feel sorry for ourselves and wallow in self-pity. This is ironic because nearly a whole book in the Bible is dedicated to the rebellious whining and moaning of the Israelites and their punishment after they left Egypt. Note that Numbers shows that even grumbling about our worries and misfortunes makes God angry.

> Now the people complained about their hardships in the hearing of the LORD, and when he heard them his anger was aroused.
> —NUMBERS 11:1, NIV

When moaning is so simple, everyone does it, and it is such an accepted part of life in today's society, why is it so serious before God? By analyzing Numbers 11, we find out it is actually rebellion against God. It takes place in our hearts as we are slowly but surely turning away from God and rejecting Him. Reasons why:

- The murmuring of God's people started off by giving in to their greedy desires. Psalm 106:14 reveals that, "In the desert they gave in to their craving; in the wasteland they put God to the test" (NIV). One result of allowing our sinful desires and lusts to become out of control is complaining. As we walk in obedience to God, He gives us the power to dominate them, but when we rebel, they become exposed and we will start whining about them and God.
- His people were nostalgic about their old life of slavery in Egypt and they desired it, believing it was better than what their new lives in the desert offered them. Of course, it was not superior; they had been deceived and were blinded by their yearnings. When we look back to our old life, we might be tempted to idealize the past and wish to return there, i.e., give up our hope in Jesus to live as the world does. The Israelites wished for different, richer foods, representing their covetousness and desires that please the flesh. They grumbled, "If only we had meat to eat! We remember the fish we ate in Egypt at no cost—also the cucumbers, melons, leeks, onions and garlic" (Num. 11:4–5, NIV). However, as slaves in Egypt, such food would not have been a common meal.

Through this new trial God had given them, they romanticized their slavery and longed for it. They rejected what God had done for them and wanted to choose slavery over freedom. When we start to complain, we reject His atoning work by longing for our old captivity over the freedom Christ has given us.

- Complaining tests God. Jacob's descendants asserted unbelief and did not trust God. They doubted His power and goodness to change the situation and provide meat. In the same way, we challenge God when we kick up a fuss.

- We complain because we forget what God has done for us, as the Israelites promptly forgot too. As we take our gaze off Jesus and His great mercies and concentrate on ourselves and our problems in our own little world, we are forgetting the good and great things God has done for us.

- Complaining is a form of disobedience. In Exodus 16:4, God revealed that He would test the Israelites' obedience by providing them with manna. Through their whining and therefore rejection of His provision, they failed the test of faith and obedience.

- Protesting demonstrates a lack of gratitude. In Numbers 11:20, God accuses the Israelites of being ungrateful in their wailing. They took His blessings for granted and discarded them. Likewise, we must always remember to show a grateful heart before God. (See the section entitled "Thanksgiving" in Chapter 11.)

The Hebrews' groaning had very serious consequences. When their journey to the Promised Land should have taken around two weeks, it took them forty years. God in His mercy allows us to learn from them. When we moan and grumble, neither will we grow, mature, or move on in our spiritual walk. Complaining stunts our growth and makes us stay in the same place, going around in circles. It is very difficult for groaners to win spiritual battles and progress in the faith. The muttering of the Israelites led them to lose faith in God. The result? A whole generation of Israelites is buried in the desert of Sinai.

The Bible explains that what we say comes naturally according to what is in our heart.

> A good man out of the good treasure of his heart brings forth good; and an evil man out of the evil treasure of his heart brings forth evil. For out of the abundance of the heart his mouth speaks.
>
> —LUKE 6:45

This means that whoever speaks about adultery all the time is probably involved in it, and whoever always talks about sex has a problem in that area. If someone never stops mentioning a certain sin, it is likely he or she is dabbling in it.

Therefore, the words we ought to have on our lips should be words of wisdom, helpful and a profitable to everyone around us. The only way to know what wise words to say to people is to ask God to place His wisdom in us and to diligently study the Word of God. Everything we need to equip us for every situation in life and advice on how to deal with every type of person we will ever meet is all found in the Bible. With the help of the Holy Spirit, we do not need any other book or set of principles to become as wise as Solomon.

The type of comments we should always have on our lips are to be positive ones, whatever the situation (1 Cor. 4:13). Even in the direst circumstances, we need to be optimistic and be full of God's joy, always looking on the bright side. Those whose lips bear negative fruit become depressive people and even dull company. As the light of the world, this must never be the case for a Christian. Our lips are to be used to glorify God and to lift to Him a sacrifice of praise. In the words of James, "Out of the same mouth proceed blessing and cursing. My brethren, these things ought not to be so" (James 3:10). Therefore our mouths should be applied to honor God and bless our neighbor.

A Sacrifice of Praise

Through Jesus, therefore, let us continually offer to God a sacrifice of praise—the fruit of lips that confess his name.

—Hebrews 13:15, NIV

Under the Old Testament laws, God's people had to offer Him sacrifices consisting of material substances. However, under the new covenant, through the blood of Jesus, which covers our sins and makes us in right standing before God, we no longer have to do this. Instead, as the writer of Hebrews tells us, the only sacrifice left to make is a continual sacrifice of praise.

Praise is the exaltation of God with words. It is expressing the glory of God and includes thanking Him. (See the section entitled "Thanksgiving" in Chapter 11.) It is often a public confession of love and commitment to God, even before unbelievers (Ps. 9:11). In Jeremiah 33:11, God predicts His people will sing the following praises to him: "Give thanks to the LORD Almighty, for the LORD is good; his love endures forever" (NIV).

Praise is often directed at God for His work in our lives, both personally and generally; that is, for showing us His redemption and unfailing love as well as for our own personal and specific experiences with Him. Just who He is, is cause for praise. His goodness, His mercy, His comfort and compassion to us, His greatness, His righteousness, His Word, His faithfulness, His deliverances, His creation, His salvation, and His grace, to name but a few. Admiring God in the Bible is performed with music and instruments, singing new and spiritual songs, clapping hands (Ps. 47:1), shouting for joy (Ps. 33:3), and calling all nations to extol God (Ps. 148:11–12). Too often nowadays we sing praise songs in church that, instead of focusing on the Lord, center on ourselves. Even if the music is asking for wholesome things from Him, the essence should still be Him and not about us receiving from Him.

The Bible's greatest single source of tribute to God is the Book of Psalms. It captures intimate meditation on God, His characteristics, and work. The psalms express many different approaches to praising Him—some shout

(Ps. 47:1) or weep before Him (Ps. 39:12), others sing songs of victory or call everything with or without breath to exalt His holy name (Ps. 150 and 98:8). Some psalms of praise are joyful and invigorating; others are solemn and profound (Ps. 6:6–9). There is a time to glorify God in all different ways. Those who praise Him during times of difficulty and sadness are those who are more likely to endure to the end of the race.

Within the psalms of praise, a very real danger is nearly always present, namely the psalmists' enemies and the precarious situation the worshiper is in at the hands of his adversary. This often sets the scene for adoring God. God is the psalmists' only source of protection and hope; their joy and peace in the Lord is the only thing that guarantees them justice and victory. With their hope in Him, the only thing left to do is relish His love and presence.

With this in mind, one function of praise is that of a sharp sword to fight battles with. Whenever we are in spiritual warfare, whether it be contending against a sinful desire, temptation to do wrong, or fighting off evil thoughts, in addition to answering the devil with the Word of God, we need to focus our mind on God and start to applaud and adore Him with our thoughts and mouth. This military tactic is demonstrated literally by King Jehoshaphat in 2 Chronicles 20:21–23. Jehoshaphat assigned men to praise God for His holiness. Verse 22 tells us, "Now when they began to sing and to praise, the LORD set ambushes against the people of Ammon, Moab, and Mount Seir, who had come against Judah; and they were defeated."

While in prison, Paul and Silas also recognized the value of this strategy. Instead of complaining, cursing, and lamenting their unfortunate situation, which is often the easiest attitude to take, they prayed and sung hymns (Acts 16:25). What a victorious position! Praise gives us the strength to get through difficult times. It focuses our thoughts on God and not on the problem or affliction at hand.

Another aspect of the power of praise is that it brings about a greater intimacy between God and the adorer. Through lifting God up in prayer and before people, we are declaring His worth and are therefore growing in His love. Admiring God also strengthens our prayers. After Solomon offered a thousand burnt offerings to the Lord, God appeared to him and let him have one request (1 Kings 3:4–5). Praise is so powerful that God purposely uses the instinctive adoration of little children to silence His enemies (Matt. 21:16).

Jesus ordered His disciples to stay in Jerusalem "until you have been clothed with power from on high" (Luke 24:49, NIV). When this power fell on them, it was partly manifested by the gift of speaking praises to God in other languages (Acts 2:4; 2:11), so speaking in tongues also brings power to our prayers as well as building up our spirit.

Praise likewise serves as medication for our soul. It cleanses our mind of evil and ungodly desires, replacing them with God's truth. Instead of having a heart full of gossip and critical, mundane thoughts, when we focus on the Lord and offer Him a sacrifice of praise, it actually remedies a dirty mouth.

Jesus sung a hymn with His disciples at the Last Supper (Mark 14:26) because united adoration brings about closer fellowship among the body of believers (Rom. 15:5–6). When there is a lack of praise to God in our lives, it may be a danger sign that we are no longer "hot" for God, our First Love.

ANGER

> But I say, if you are even angry with someone, you are subject to judgment! If you call someone an idiot, you are in danger of being brought before the court. And if you curse someone, you are in danger of the fires of hell.
>
> —MATTHEW 5:22, NLT

Subject to judgment means that depending on the reason for our anger, we will either be found righteous or condemned. For the times when we are justified (i.e., when the root cause of our wrath involves a sin against God), Jesus teaches that we still should never lose our temper, unless we get cross under the direction of the Holy Spirit, as did Saul in 1 Samuel 11:6. Losing our temper means we fail to keep control of our senses, and we will always say things we regret later. In fact, fury destroys the angry person more than those it is directed toward.

When somebody's mistake or incompetence costs us time, frustration, and money, we need to be careful not to show wrath. For instance, being woken up in the middle of the night by someone's thoughtlessness, however frustrating it may be, should not lead us into anger. Having to wait longer in a traffic jam or line than normal should not make us cross. We must view it as an opportunity to pray longer, have fellowship or witness with whomever is in the car, or listen to a wholesome radio program. Becoming enraged with children for doing something they do not understand is not justified; instead, it should be a moment seized to teach them something new.

It can be difficult to curb our anger as we feel it welling up inside us, but we must remind ourselves of scripture such as Proverbs 30:33, "Surely the churning of milk bringeth forth butter, and the wringing of the nose bringeth forth blood: so the forcing of wrath bringeth forth strife" (KJV), and Proverbs 21:23, "Whoever guards his mouth and tongue Keeps his soul from troubles." When we feel rage boiling over, we must suppress it in the fear of the Lord and remember that a shut mouth is better than an open one. We need to be careful not to sin by letting anger gain control over us, but we must subdue it so it will not lead us into sin.

Anger with a justified cause is acceptable, but it still needs to be controlled; otherwise, it can very easily lead us into sin. Anger is only righteous when the cause is directly related to sinning against God (not a sin against ourselves). Under no circumstances are we, in our just anger, allowed to insult, mock, or judge another person. Even in our godly anger, we are required to show restraint. In verse 9 of Jude, Michael the archangel did not even criticize the devil, but said, "The Lord rebuke you!" as they were arguing about the whereabouts of Moses' corpse.

In Psalm 4, David demonstrates godly anger because the people around him sought dishonesty and pagan gods rather than the Lord. Even though he was justified in his anger before God, he still warned himself in verse 4, "In your anger do not sin; when you are on your beds, search your hearts and be silent" (NIV). His advice is not to act violently, nor with shouting, but to go and relax to calm our nerves and then examine our innermost conscience and hidden intentions and attitudes to extract the reason behind the anger and make sure we are not displeasing God. David's counsel is to keep quiet when feeling righteous anger. Paul uses the first part of this verse in Ephesians 4:26 in the context of Christians who do not get along with each other; they must control themselves and not remain angry for long.

I have seen so many Christians argue and bicker about worldly and worthless things. At the time, everybody seemed oblivious to the fact that it was the devil sowing his seeds and that it was not a fruit of God's Spirit. Nobody seemed concerned that we should have been rebuking it and praying for God's deliverance and breakthrough. Paul speaks about those who bicker when he wrote, "For you are still carnal. For where there are envy, strife, and divisions among you, are you not carnal and behaving like mere men?" (1 Cor. 3:3). As Christians, we have died with Christ, and therefore have departed from sin. We should be living in the Spirit, not alive in the flesh. Paul tries to get the Corinthians to turn away from quarrels that do not need to be decided for the good of the believing community but encourages them to look at the bigger picture and see that they are allowing the devil to sow discord among them.

Ephraim was quick to anger and judged Gideon because of his apparent failure to call them for their services while fighting against Midian. Gideon's kind reply pacified a raging tribe. Instead of inventing excuses or verbally attacking them in return, he controlled his reaction and focused on their victory and on the positive outcome they had achieved. Wisely, he subsided their indignation by complimenting them, at the expense of himself (Judges 8:2–3). As James recommends in James 1:19–20, we must also be "swift to hear, slow to speak, slow to wrath; for the wrath of man does not produce the righteousness of God" in the same way Gideon was.

Four chapters later in Judges, exactly the same accusations arise against the new Judge of Israel, Jephthah. Ephraim, without thinking about the consequences, launches allegations and threats they are unable to fulfill. With no thought as to how they would carry out their menaces and blinded by pride, they vented their foolish anger. As Ephraim still hadn't learned the ways of the Lord, God permitted the slaughter of forty-two thousand Ephramites that day. The next time they were not called to fight, they surely gave their feelings a second thought and decided to let the injustice pass. As Proverbs 29:11 demonstrates, "A fool vents all his feelings [as in the case of Ephraim], But a wise man holds them back [as in Gideon's case]."

Chapter 8

SEPARATION FROM THE WORLD

*Do not love the world or the things in the world. If anyone loves
the world, the love of the Father is not in him. For all that is in the
world—the lust of the flesh, the lust of the eyes, and the pride of life—is
not of the Father but is of the world. And the world is passing away,
and the lust of it; but he who does the will of God abides forever.*

1 John 2:15–17

F OR A CHRISTIAN to be a Christian, there must be distinction from
the world. By *the world*, John refers to our fallen way of life and
society on Earth. It is hostile to God, has Satan as its prince, and its
constitution is against God's. It is represented by its worldly values, worldly
wisdom, worldly pleasures; basically everything the flesh delights in, the
world honors. But God does not (Luke 16:15). Paul explains *worldliness* by
describing what he and Titus were like before becoming born again: "For we
ourselves were also once foolish, disobedient, deceived, serving various lusts
and pleasures, living in malice and envy, hateful and hating one another"
(Titus 3:3).

Noah's ark represents our salvation, and the Flood, our baptism (1 Pet.
3:21). Noah entered the boat and was separated from the rest of the world
by the floodwaters. In the same way that Noah was in the boat, we are in
Christ; and we are detached and different than the world, just as Noah was

set apart from it when he was in the ark. The waterlogged globe around him symbolized the world around us, flooded with lies, hatred, injustice, corruption, and violence. In the same way that baptism typifies our washing away of sin and being born into a new life, Noah's world was cleansed from sin with the spring and rainwater. Therefore, he disembarked into a changed habitat, just as we cross the threshold into a new life after baptism. It was by faith that Noah believed God and built the ark (Heb. 11:7). He was segregated and chosen by God from his whole generation. And it is by faith that we are also not conformed to this world (Rom. 12:1) and are chosen (1 Pet. 2:9) and made different in God's sight.

Because of this new life and holy segregation we have been ordained into, God's grace now "teaches us to say 'No' to ungodliness and worldly passions, and to live self-controlled, upright and godly lives in this present age, while we wait for the blessed hope—the glorious appearing of our great God and Savior, Jesus Christ" (Titus 2:12–13, NIV). This means that we now should not show the same depth of interest as the world regarding their music, films, books, technology, games, shopping, clothes, fashion, art, dating, sports, amusements, celebrities, thought-pools, and ways of life. I am not saying it is wrong to partake in these pursuits and affairs; rather, as Christians our interest is bound to be less and never extreme or obsessive because of our eternal hope and our vigilance for Jesus' return.

Our central focus in life is supposed to be on God, His truth, and how to live according to His will. We must also patiently wait for His second coming. All of our attitudes and our whole outlook on life are to be disunited from the world because we have been raised into a brand-new life with Jesus. Paul puts it clearly in Galatians 6:14: "The world has been crucified to me, and I to the world." So, we will no longer boast about places we have been to or what we have achieved or done; rather, we will only ever boast in what Jesus has done. Feats are no longer important to us because the things of God are now of more worth.

It is impossible to be completely separated from the world because we are living in it. However, this distinction refers to having a radically different thought pattern from society's. What the world at large honors, including vanity, pride, large amounts of wealth, hope placed in our achievements and possessions, sexual pleasure outside of marriage, being in control of one's own life and destiny, are to be contrasted with our way of living. Peter calls Christians to live as aliens and strangers on Earth, so that pagans will give God glory (1 Pet. 2:11–12, NIV). We are to live as foreigners here because this is where sin reigns and flourishes, not God's ways and His righteousness. Looking back in Israel's history, the Mosaic Law regarding property rights uncovers that even then God required His people to consider themselves nonresidents on Earth: "The land must not be sold permanently, because the land is mine and you are but aliens and my tenants" (Lev. 25:23, NIV).

In Colossians 2:8, Paul touches on the danger of placing confidence in the ways of the world, including man-made tradition and philosophy, instead of trusting in biblical wisdom and knowledge. Today, as Christians we must be wary of following the thinking of the world, which relies on one's own efforts to feel whole and satisfied in life and does not depend on God for spiritual fulfillment. It is fatal if we seek to fulfill ourselves through our jobs, our families, our holidays, how much we earn, our hobbies, worldly entertainment, our cars, houses, or material goods. The Christians in Colosse were also seeking fullness of life in the wrong things; therefore, God channeled their thinking toward the fullness they had already received in Christ (Col. 2:10).

One worldly concept to which many Christians have succumbed is that we need to learn to love and accept ourselves as we are and that some of us need professional or spiritual treatment to "cure" feelings of self-rejection and self-hatred. This may include the "need" to complete a therapeutic or psychiatric process, also called self-help courses, to be able to understand and properly care for ourselves. Feelings of self-worth and self-value are promoted, going directly against Jesus' teaching on humility. This is exceedingly cunning because telling everyone not to hate themselves is an attractive and nice-sounding theory. However, it undermines His divine work on two scales.

Firstly, this completely challenges the Lord's requirement that we treat and love one another as we love ourselves (Gal. 5:14; Lev. 19:18). This means that we all do already love ourselves, except for some mentally challenged people. Who hopes for illnesses and bad things to fall upon themselves? Nobody. Why? Because we all spontaneously love ourselves. It is something natural that God in His awesome power has placed inside each one of us (Eph. 5:29).

Secondly, often the way we are is not how God wants us to be, for example, if we are struggling with a sin and haven't overcome it yet, such as masturbation, gluttony, or gossiping. No one can claim to be perfect. If they do they are probably guilty of pride. God is working in us, and we "are being transformed into his likeness" (2 Cor. 3:18, NIV). So teaching people self-esteem and that they don't need to change interrupts God's perfecting work in us and instead causes us to concentrate on our ego, forgetting that we are subject to God's will. This is not to mention taking the focus away from holiness.

Similarly, the Israelites repeatedly forfeited God's favor to be more like the world. Because their hearts were not truly converted toward Him and His goodness, His special favor and treatment became dull to them. He became boring, and His laws, monotonous. They gave in to their envy and lusts and idolized the governing system of other nations instead of accepting Jehovah as King and Samuel the prophet as a national leader. To them, foreign peoples seemed so glorious in battle with a king as head of state (1 Sam. 8:19–20). Even though the Hebrews were warned they would be worse off with a king, conformity to the world was their ultimate aspiration. Instead of trusting in God Almighty, whom they could not see, it required much less effort and faith to succumb to their carnality and trust in a man whom they could see.

All this can happen in the lives of us today as Christians. It can be very easy to stop making an effort to pray, read the Bible, seek God, and live righteously. We then look around us, expose ourselves too much to the world's culture and ways of life, and also start to wish we lived in the same way. The essence of Israel's sin in requesting a king was the rejection of their covenant with the Lord, who Himself was their Monarch and Protector. In exactly the same way, we can reject our covenant with Jesus Christ as the world starts to seduce us. We then begin to forget all His benefits as we renounce Him as King of our lives. We lose sight of God's grace and goodness and make ourselves vulnerable to what we see around us, prostituting ourselves to worldly things. Instead of fixing our eyes on our eternal reward and renewing our mind with an eternal perspective, we allow our eyes to wander toward this world and glory here on Earth, just as God's chosen people repeatedly did, from their freedom from slavery in Egypt right up to the present time.

In 1 Samuel 8:11–18, Samuel warns Israel of the downside of having an earthly king. Instead of having a better quality of life, which is what they believed a king would bring, the result would be trouble and strife. As slaves of the king, he would abuse them and their belongings for his own personal use. The world also does this to us when we decide to trust in it rather than God for our security. We become the most wretched slaves, so much so that hopefully we, too, will cry out to God for relief from the world and its ways, as Samuel predicted the Israelis would (1 Sam. 8:18). It is impossible to live for God and at the same time be loved and accepted by the world. James reminds us, "Do you not know that friendship with the world is enmity with God? Whoever therefore wants to be a friend of the world makes himself an enemy of God" (James 4:4). We have to choose either one or the other.

Christians should expect to be hated by some of those around us who, as they observe we are different and despise us (1 John 3:13; John 15:18–19). Although it may be hard, especially from people we know and love, Jesus stresses that these instances should be moments of joy, not sorrow (Matt. 5:12). We must remember that on the Day of Judgment, we will be victorious, as the Spirit who lives in us is greater than the spirit who lives in the world (1 John 4:4). (See the section entitled "Endurance in Suffering" in Chapter 13.)

Whoever carries out the will of God is someone who has separated themselves from worldliness and abides by the Holy Spirit. If you don't know whether you have done God's will or not, it may be that you haven't. Those who do His will are those who live according to His precepts and constantly seek Him and ask Him to guide and lead them throughout life. They do not make any decisions without prayerfully asking God which path is the right one. If you have not done His will, do not worry; as long as you are still living, there is still time to repent and submit to Him.

This submission is key. Some people teach that we need to follow our heart's desires, because God will put His plans inside us. Yes, He sometimes does that, but not always. It is a real test of faith when we have one aspiration and God tells us to do something completely different.

MIXING WITH UNBELIEVERS

> To the weak I became as weak, that I might win the weak. I have become all things to all men, that I might by all means save some.
> —1 CORINTHIANS 9:22

We are in the world but not part of it. Therefore, we are always mixing with non-Christians to whom we are called to preach the gospel (Matt. 28:19–20) and be light (Luke 11:33). Paul, an example for us to follow, sought in every opportunity to be a witness to all who crossed his path. Always concerned with the salvation of others, he explained he acted as a Gentile to the Gentiles, a Jew to the Jews, and oppressed to the oppressed in order to open up each person's mind to the truth of the gospel (1 Cor. 9:20–22). In his words, he makes himself everyone's servant to win as many over to God as possible (v. 19).

In today's society, this would be acting as a sports fan to sports fans, as a member of the working class to the working class, as a hippie to hippies, as a family-orientated person to those who are family-orientated, as career-focused to the career-focused, a skater to the skaters, middle class to the middle class, and so forth, to be an effective witness. All this must be done without forgetting God's high standard of holiness He requires from us and without idolizing such ways of life or finding fulfillment in them. We should moderately adapt to the people around us so as to faithfully radiate Christ's beauty.

Paul also left the Corinthians with several instructions regarding relationships with unbelievers. He wrote, "If someone who isn't a believer asks you home to dinner, accept the invitation if you want to" (1 Cor. 10:27, NLT). Although Paul is writing about food sacrificed to idols, we can still learn that it is acceptable to eat with unbelievers. However, in a surprising twist, Paul interdicts eating with those who claim to be Christian but in fact are not: "You are not to associate with anyone who claims to be a believer yet indulges in sexual sin, or is greedy, or worships idols, or is abusive, or is a drunkard, or cheats people. Don't even eat with such people" (1 Cor. 5:11, NLT). We are not to tolerate unbelievers who pretend they are followers of Christ.

Paul, writing under the direction of the Holy Spirit, clearly forbids the saints to marry non-Christians:

> Don't team up with those who are unbelievers. How can righteousness be a partner with wickedness? How can light live with darkness? What harmony can there be between Christ and the devil? How can a believer be a partner with an unbeliever? And what union can there be between God's temple and idols?
> —2 CORINTHIANS 6:14–16, NLT

Paul cites Isaiah 52:11 a verse later when he repeats, "Therefore, come out from among unbelievers, and separate yourselves from them, says the LORD" (NLT). If you married an unbeliever in ignorance of this, do not feel condemned about it, and thank God for them always. Paul admonishes people who are married to nonbelievers in verses 12 to 16 to stay married if that is what the unbelieving spouse wants. But if you still have the choice, you need to act in obedience to God and marry a Christian rather than a disbeliever. Remember that Solomon's pagan wives led him astray from the path of righteousness (1 Kings 11:4).

While it is important to have non-Christian friends to whom we can be a light in this dark world, we need to be careful of hanging around with those who have a spiritually negative influence on us. We must to strive to make our holy witness overpower their evil influence as we are praying for their conversion. However, if their bad character is having a detrimental effect on us, we are told to "have no fellowship with the unfruitful works of darkness, but rather expose them. For it is shameful even to speak of those things which are done by them in secret" (Eph. 5:11–12). We must watch how much time we spend with these sorts of people, because the world shouldn't affect us; rather, we should sway it. (See the section entitled "Shining Out" in Chapter 11.)

We also need to be careful not to associate with their sinful lifestyle and guard ourselves against being led astray by them.

> You therefore, beloved, since you know this beforehand, beware lest you also fall from your own steadfastness, being led away with the error of the wicked; but grow in the grace and knowledge of our Lord and Savior Jesus Christ.
>
> —2 PETER 3:17–18

We must be wise when we spend time with those who do not share our faith and keep a check on our spiritual growth. If we feel our closeness to God weakening around such people, it may be a warning to spend more time in fellowship with believers rather than in the company of darkness. Psalm 106:34–38 also advises against mingling too much with non-Christians because of the danger of adopting their practices and losing our spirituality. It is therefore foolish to have very close unbelieving friends.

One area where God's people should not partner with non-Christians is in business enterprises. Business partnerships with nonbelievers always caused retribution and failings in Israel's history. Take the God-fearing, religiously zealous king of Judah, Jehoshaphat, as an example. He was such a star that he personally visited his people to persuade them to follow the Lord (2 Chron. 19:4). Today's equivalent would be if a budding evangelist became the leader of a nation. He was so godly that the heathen nations around Judah feared the Lord (2 Chron. 17:10) and they took him tribute.

Jehoshaphat did, however, fall down in one area. He formed a business partnership with a man "guilty of wickedness" (2 Chron. 20:35, NIV). Ahaziah was a fellow Israelite, the king of Israel, but this was not enough in God's eyes. Jehoshaphat was only allowed to form alliances with those who really did fear God, not with the wicked. The two invested in the nautical commerce together, but God's judgment was around the corner. The ships were smashed, and nothing came of the relationship. In the same way, if we form a confederation with someone who does not serve God, we may find that the Lord will work against us, too.

INTOLERANCE OF FALSE CHRISTIANS; TOLERANCE OF BACKSLIDDEN CHRISTIANS

> This know also, that in the last days perilous times shall come. For men shall be lovers of their own selves, covetous, boasters, proud, blasphemers, disobedient to parents, unthankful, unholy, Without natural affection, trucebreakers, false accusers, incontinent, fierce, despisers of those that are good, Traitors, heady, highminded, lovers of pleasures more than lovers of God; Having a form of godliness, but denying the power thereof: from such turn away.
>
> —2 TIMOTHY 3:1–5, KJV

I believe this passage refers to people in the church today because it mentions in verse 5 that they have a form of godliness, possibly linking it with the wolves in sheep's clothing Jesus talks about in Matthew 7:15–20. These are people who pretend to be genuine Christians in order to destroy churches and people's faith, consciously or unconsciously. By their fruit, one can tell they are not authentic believers and are used by the devil for his purposes. They cause trouble and strife within the church. Jesus calls them "false prophets" (Matt. 7:15, KJV). Because of how real and near the threat of such damaging false Christians are to the church, Paul felt the urgency strongly enough to tearfully forewarn the church in Ephesus about it continuously for three years (Acts 20:31). Paul, inspired by the Holy Spirit, charges us to steer clear of such people and in fact turn away from them. We also need to be on guard and watchful for people like this who want to take our salvation away from us by deception.

We need to be especially wary of institutions, nations, organizations, powers, authorities, and churches that on the outside look like kind, gentle, and innocent, even religious; but in fact, they speak "as a dragon" (Rev. 13:11, KJV). This is a characteristic of the second beast in Revelation, which will come out of the earth. The prophecy that it will speak with a drag-on's voice means that instead of speaking truth, the beast will speak lies to deceive the people. It will claim it has been sent by God but will not practice or obey His Word. It will exercise exactly what the Word of God condemns, in line with being a wolf in sheep's clothing.

Believers need discernment and knowledge to know whom to accept and support and whom to avoid. With regard to a Christian in sin, who is not necessarily a wolf in sheep's clothing, just a brother who has made an error of judgment, Jesus' advice in Matthew 18:15–17 is that the first time the brother sins, we should privately point out his mistake in love. Paul calls this restoring "in the spirit of meekness" (Gal. 6:1, KJV). If, however, he does not take note, he should be corrected in front of one or two more people from the church. If he still does not change his ways, he needs to be confronted by the church. If he does not accept this discipline, he should be removed from fellowship but nevertheless still treated with love. The level of holiness and purity within churches is to be so high that the tolerance of sin must be zero. Jesus does not point out the type of sin in this context, so it should be regarded as any sin, whether it be dishonesty, pride, selfishness, or sexual immorality, etc.

The way we are to treat false Christians is very different from how the Bible teaches we are to interact with genuinely backslidden ones. The lost son in Luke 15:11–32, a backslider, reminisced about his father's house and remem-bered his father's servants because they had been well-treated there. This situation should be the same with sidetracked people who have left the church to follow their own ways instead of God's. We must make them feel welcome and loved by God's people, giving them a positive image of the church so that when they despair, they will feel drawn to God's people and therefore to Him. Even if they know church is a place where they will be corrected, with good sense they will realize it is for their own benefit. God willing, they will see correction as given with an attitude of love and out of a desire for their spiritual success. This way it is much easier for an ex-believer to find their way back on the right path. In 1 John 5:16, John also exhorts us to pray for brothers in sin, if it is not "a sin that leads to death" (NIV).

Paul implores us to be wary of deceitful teachers behind the pulpit.

> Now I urge you, brethren, note those who cause divisions and offenses, contrary to the doctrine which you learned, and avoid them. For those who are such do not serve our Lord Jesus Christ, but their own belly, and by smooth words and flattering speech deceive the hearts of the simple.
>
> —ROMANS 16:17–18

The term *false teachers* (2 Pet. 2:1) also refers to preachers who especially seek to gain financially from their sermons or seminars (1 Tim. 6:5). Jesus says, "The worker is worth his keep," in Matthew 10:10 (NIV), so whoever commits themselves to proclaiming God's truth should live off it. However, Paul is saying that whoever preaches exclusively to try and get rich is corrupt and two-faced. John advises his readers not to offer hospitality or welcome such people (2 John 10–11) so as not to share in their evil work.

Balaam taught Balak how to lead Israel astray (Num. 31:16). He knew their weaknesses were idolatry and sexual temptation, so he abused this knowledge to gain wealth. Enemies of the gospel will always attack the body of Christ where it is weakest. Revelation 2:14–16 warns about tolerance of people like Balaam. Repentance is needed just for putting up with such attitudes, because we should never associate with those who make Christians fall or who compromise God's truth.

In New Testament times, the Pharisees and Sadducees represented those who taught false truths about God (Matt. 16:12). Jesus called them hypocrites (Matt. 15:7), and He also warned believers to be aware of their teachings in Matthew 16:6.

Today, Pharisees and Sadducees still exist, although they no longer have that name. They are people in the church who call themselves Christians but hold the same hypocrisy of the Pharisees and Sadducees. They are people who either pretend to be believers, or they actually think they are and are genuinely deluded. They think that by fulfilling the easier truths of God's Law, such as not telling lies, not murdering, not stealing, reading the Bible, praying, loving their families, being honest with their taxes, and not taking drugs, they are Christians.

However, when it comes to fulfilling God's harder commandments involving holy living and holiness in their thought life, they fall down. For example, they may be unable to restrain from lust, pornography, greed, and self-indulgence. They are incapable of loving their enemies and turning the other cheek (Matt. 5:39). They enjoy being part of the world, and the world loves and accepts them. They love this recognition. They may not commit physical adultery, but they commit spiritual adultery in their hearts. Jesus says of them, "Woe to you, teachers of the law and Pharisees, you hypocrites! You clean the outside of the cup and dish, but inside they are full of greed and self-indulgence" (Matt. 23:25). "Cleansing outside of the cup" nowadays refers to looking like a Christian externally, going to church and leading a seemingly honest life. Jesus warns that sorrow awaits these people (Matt. 23:13). In order to be clean from the inside, we need to lead a life of holiness presented up to God as a sweet-smelling offering.

After receiving God's salvation and goodness and after a while of attending church and Bible study, it is easy to get so used to hearing God's truth over and over that it no longer sounds new. We can become so exceedingly accustomed to all the stories in the Bible and the letters of Paul that we become distant and stop listening to God's voice through His Word; we always think we know what will come next. We may think of ourselves as mature believers, and without realizing it, we may turn Bible reading and church attendance into our religion and actually mentally switch off at church and while reading the Scriptures. Instead of listening to the sermon or taking in God's Word, we accommodate fleshly thoughts and think about worldly things. At the end of the day, we believe we are good Christians because we attend church on a regular basis, read the Bible regularly, and are friendly people, where actually we are not learning anything new and are no longer attentive to God's voice.

This is a very common and subtle way to become a Pharisee ourselves without noticing it. It can be easy to spot and judge people who we think are Pharisees and Sadducees in our church, without realizing that we have become one. Examine your own thoughts, motives, and actions, and ask yourself if you can sometimes be a hypocrite; then ask for forgiveness and God's grace to turn totally back to Him.

Chapter 9

EVANGELIZING

I F YOU MET someone who came back from the dead after three days, you would certainly listen to what they had to say! Jesus' final message after He overcame death was:

Go into all the world and preach the gospel to every creature. He who believes and is baptized will be saved; but he who does not believe will be condemned. And these signs will follow those who believe: In My name they will cast out demons; they will speak with new tongues; they will take up serpents; and if they drink anything deadly, it will by no means hurt them; they will lay hands on the sick, and they will recover.

—MARK 16:15–18

Going out and preaching the good news is the core of our calling. It is Jesus' instructions to us before and after His victory over death was won. As we remain in Him and prove ourselves to be faithful, He will in turn confirm what we say as we explain His message with many miraculous signs. This is a gift of the Spirit He grants according to His grace, so it is paramount not to forget Mark 16:20: "And the Lord worked with them and confirmed his word by the signs that accompanied it" (NIV). Jesus' message was not to just teach His truth on its own; it is to be accompanied with marvels and wonders, too—healing the sick, casting out demons, speaking in languages, protection from poisonous snakes, and the ability to drink poison without harm. Witnessing about Christ's love and the manifestation of miracles go hand in hand. They are not supposed to be separated.

When I realized that the only biblical form of evangelizing is accompanied by miracles and healing, I was stunned! Why does it not happen more today? Is it because of spiritual dryness? It could be why numbers of people becoming Christians at outreaches are sometimes smaller than what we hope for. Jesus attracted phenomenal crowds because of His reputation for healing the sick. If we also offer to heal the sick at the same time, our crowds would be exponentially larger, although we must make sure the focus is the message we transmit, rather than the signs. Jesus demonstrated this in Luke 5:14 when He told the man cured of leprosy not to spread the news about his healing. Jesus was probably concerned with the danger of being known just for the miracles, rather than the substance behind them.

Through Jesus' strong anointing and authority, the people were drawn to him (Luke 4:31). They were also pulled by His compassion toward needy people, shown through healing them and driving out evil spirits. Luke 5:16 informs us, "Jesus often withdrew to lonely places and prayed" (NIV). This was a crucial part of His ministry. It is also essential for evangelists today to be constantly seeking God for guidance and direction for every step. Another characteristic of Jesus' preaching is that He only spoke what came from His Father, not from Himself (John 7:16–17). This practice sprung from a very intimate relationship with God.

Other witnessing techniques Jesus used include going out to meet with the people and teaching them where they could be found. He met the masses where they were at both spiritually and physically rather than staying in one place, waiting for them to come to Him (Luke 4:14).

The fire-and-brimstone style of preaching, using shock tactics by telling people about hellfire and eternal damnation if they don't obey God, is often ridiculed, but we need to ask ourselves if it is biblical or not. In order to do this, and also to find out the type of message we should be relaying to not-yet-Christians, we need to be clear on the content of what Jesus communicated to the crowds. Taking the Gospels of Luke and John as a sample,

I will examine what Jesus taught to the vast hordes rather than what He mentioned in private to the disciples who were already His followers.

1) Jesus gave the common people incredibly practical and instructive commands.

- Jesus' teaching consisted of a radically different type of instruction on how to live and how to act and gave people a new and different set of values to live by that would have revolutionized their thinking and lives, if obeyed.
- Jesus did not just preach the Sermon on the Mount to His disciples, although He started off by looking at them in Luke 6:20. There were also many people present who were not His companions but were there to receive healing (Luke 6:17–18; 7:1). To this great multitude, Jesus gave advice on brotherly love and love for enemies, hypocrisy, and lending money, with exhortations to obey His teaching. None of the people present could have ever heard of such a radical attitude on human love.
- He taught the parable of the good Samaritan (Luke 10:25–37), demonstrating what real and acceptable love is in God's sight and illustrating the importance of love in action.
- He instructed the crowd in Luke 11:34–36 to be careful where to put their eyes because where one's eyes go determines if he or she has light or darkness inside.

2) Jesus gave many warnings against not believing in Him and not acting on His Word.

- In Luke 11:29–32, Jesus condemned people for not accepting His teaching.
- In the parable of the rich fool (Luke 12:13–59), Jesus warned the crowd that they should not trust in and desire money and riches; rather, they should make every effort to earn treasure in heaven. He then denounces them in verse 56 for

hypocrisy because of their lust for pleasure and possessions and because they ignored God's calling.

- Jesus' doctrine included admonitions about future condemnation and destruction for those who do not heed His words (John 12:47–48).
- Jesus forewarned that lack of repentance leads to perishing (Luke 13:3).

3) The Lord cautioned people of their spiritual state before God. He did not flower-up the gospel and pretend everything was OK for sinners.

- In John 8:34–37, He told unbelievers that everyone who sins is a slave of sin and is not a part of God's family, although He used this with a promise of freedom: "If the Son makes you free."
- Jesus told those who pretended to be religious that they were guilty of sin (John 9:41).

4) Jesus directed the anonymous crowds to repentance.

- In Matthew 4:17 and in Luke 13:1, Jesus warned them they needed to repent and turn from their sins; otherwise they would perish, meaning that a guilty verdict was on its way.

5) He spoke to the multitude about the kingdom of God.

- In Luke 9:11 and often through parables, such as the parable of the mustard tree and the parable of the lost coin.

6) Jesus never beat around the bush. He gave fair warning that it was hard to get into heaven and be His follower.

- Jesus preached the parable of the narrow door (Luke 13:24–30) in "towns and villages" (NIV). While speaking about the saving grace of God to nonbelievers, He declared that few would be saved! Jesus was blatantly honest and did not try to make the gospel and wrath of God any softer than they really were. He called those who would not receive salvation "evil-doers" here (v. 27, NIV).

- To the "large crowds traveling with Jesus" in Luke 14:25–30 (NIV), Jesus warned of the cost of becoming a disciple and cautioned them to only become Christians if they were really able to. They should not follow Him half-heartedly, only to drop out later because of lack of perseverance and dedication. He divulged that they must love Him more than anything and anyone else; if they couldn't do this, He said, then they shouldn't commit themselves to Him. He went on to mention that if they did make the commitment but then lost their saltiness, He would reject them (v. 35).

- When a rich religious man asked the way to eternal life, Jesus seized the opportunity to teach on the danger of trusting in wealth and the peril of it becoming more important to us than God (Luke 18:18–30). This is certainly not the way many of us would preach to affluent friends, although picking out their downfalls and stumbling blocks is extremely effective in getting straight to the point. This prosperous man could not be saved until he had given up his material goods.

- Jesus used the parable of the talents in Luke 19:11 to alert people that they must remain faithful to God in the administration of their gifts, or they would be punished.

- Jesus used the parable of the fig tree (Luke 13:6–9) to demonstrate to the crowd that they must produce fruit or they would be condemned, but God is mercifully patient in helping them bear fruit.

7) Jesus taught about God's love and mercy.

- He expressed God's love for the lost through the parable of the lost sheep (Luke 15:3–7), the parable of the lost coin (Luke 15:8–10), and the parable of the lost son (Luke 15:11–32).

- Jesus evangelized Nicodemus by teaching him he needed to be born again and went on to teach about the Father's love in John 3:17–18.
- Jesus taught mercy and the forgiveness of sins when He freely forgave the adulterous woman in John 8:11, with a stern warning to stop sinning.

8) Jesus revealed Himself as a miracle-maker.

- He used the phenomenon of transforming the water into wine so that the people present, who were chosen by God, would trust in Him. It also serves to show us that He provides for our needs and cares about our worries.
- Jesus raised the dead in front of believers and unbelievers.
- In most scenes with Jesus in the Gospel of Luke, He heals or casts out demons, which formed a large part of His ministry.
- The feeding of the four thousand and five thousand show Him as one who meets and therefore understands the basic human necessities.

9) Jesus always claimed to meet spiritual needs and give out spiritual blessings.

- He revealed to the Samaritan woman (John 4:10–13) that He had the power to prevent people from ever becoming spiritually thirsty again. He professed to be able to refresh her in a spiritual and everlasting way that would lead her into eternal life. He promised her spiritual and everlasting benefits. The incredible thing about this particular case is that no miracle was performed. This underscores the point that it was through Jesus' words, not physical provision, that the people

believed in Him. Notice also that this incident involves a
woman preaching.

> Many of the Samaritans of that city believed in Him because of
> the word of the woman who testified.... And many more believed
> because of His own word.
>
> —JOHN 4:39, 41

- In John 7:37–38, Jesus preached the same thing to the crowds
  on the last day of the Passover. He promised spiritual fulfillment in life through the Holy Spirit and an eternal reward.
- He promised freedom from sin to those who believe in Him
  (John 8:32).
- He assured eternal life for those who have faith in Him (John
  12:44–45).

10) Jesus uses the truth to evangelize.

- He preached about who He is to attract the crowds. With His
  seven "I am" descriptions in John, Jesus pointed to Himself
  as God and as the meaning of life everyone is looking for.

With Jesus as the perfect example of how we should live our lives on this
earth, we should imitate Him and also reflect what He preached in our own
evangelism to unbelievers rather than addressing what we think nonbelievers would like to hear. Jesus' good news preaching is full of admonitions
for those who do not do God's will, calling for the repentance of sins; revelation about the truth and who God is; what He can do for the people (always
spiritual, not material); and examples of the kind of life those who follow
Christ are expected to live.

Unfortunately, the Bible has been used as propaganda to attract and almost
trick people into becoming Christian. We sometimes present an adulter-
ated gospel so as to "win more souls" just to get a larger congregation, as if

God needs a little help along the way. Joshua did not push the Israelites into following God. Instead, he gave them the free option of choosing which god to follow (Josh. 24:15–22). He was aware what would happen if they forsook the Almighty. His wrath and jealousy would turn against them. The people had to actually convince Joshua it was the Lord they wanted to serve! We need to be careful to present pure gospel truth to people and encourage them to follow God, but with the positives and negatives clearly laid out. (For example, there is the reward of eternal life, but converts need to leave their old ways of life behind.)

In the same way, we can overemphasize the positive part of the message of the gospel and not talk or teach enough about the harder parts to accept, such as the inevitability of suffering as a Christian (Rom. 8:17) or dying to ourselves daily (Luke 9:23). Too often, God's provisions and divine help become the focus, as we concentrate on the satisfaction and protection God promises us. Of course, it is part of God's Word and needs to be taught, but we sometimes seem to have lost the central emphasis of the truth of the Scriptures to this prosperity and blessing preaching. We draw people to Christ through promises of a better and easier life, forgetting repentance, forgetting that Jesus demands sacrifice on our part and to love Him more than our families and friends (Luke 14:26).

We need to be careful not to transmit a man-made gospel just to draw as many followers as possible, promising material goods and an easy life. Instead, we should be teaching any possible new converts things such as what God's Son taught to a crowd in Luke 12:15:

> Watch out! Be on your guard against all kinds of greed; a man's
> life does not consist in the abundance of his possessions. (NIV)

In lieu of using material blessings to entice people to Him, He did the opposite. Christ warned whoever seeks only the cares, riches, and delights in life that these things do not give fruit with perfection. We need to avoid teaching people that all God wants to do in their life is bless them and make them prosper financially if they trust in Him, omitting the message of holiness. God loves the world, yes, and those who become Christians need to know that God wants their heart, so their ways and old life will need to change dramatically as they take up their cross daily and die to their own desires and aspirations. They need to know that Jesus says in John 12:25, "He who loves his life will lose it, and he who hates his life in this world will keep it for eternal life."

If we want to be a faithful testimony to our contemporaries, we should mirror Jesus' words and teachings, just as Peter did. Peter's preaching method was full of cautions, too.

> With many other words he warned them; and he pleaded with them, "Save yourselves from this corrupt generation."
> —ACTS 2:40, NIV

We need to take a look at the Bible afresh and actually see what it says without adapting it to what we want to hear.

While many of us may never get the chance to evangelize on a mass scale, there is still personal evangelism to our non-Christian friends, family, and acquaintances that we are all responsible for before God. First Peter 3:15 directs us to always be ready to share our faith: "Always be prepared to give an answer to everyone who asks you to give the reason for the hope that you have" (NIV). This can be carried out in a very practical way by prayerfully writing down in a structured order how and why you became a Christian. Don't forget to practice and memorize what you have written! We should likewise be prepared to answer questions that may be raised relating to our personal testimony. Being prepared will also help ensure that your presentation is done with gentleness and respect.

It is also a good idea to rehearse explaining the gospel in a nutshell, with the help of the Holy Spirit. While talking to Cornelius and his household in Acts 10:42–43, Peter imparts what he understands as talking to others about the gospel: "And He commanded us to preach to the people, and to testify that it is He who was ordained by God to be Judge of the living and the dead. To Him all the prophets witness that, through His name, whoever believes in Him will receive remission of sins." Another scheme is to design a flyer or tract a with a simple but powerful gospel message and always have some on the ready to hand out anywhere we go. See www.wordsarenotenoughministry.org for ideas for flyers.

Possibly one of the most common forms of opposition to the Christian faith in the Western world is the question of why God allows suffering. Again, we must have some sort of answer up our sleeves so as to not be caught off guard and let a skeptic think they are more clever than we are. One brief explanation to this sensitive issue could be that when God made the world, He didn't actually plan suffering to be a part of it. Because God loved His creation, He gave us free will; and it was humans who chose to sin against Him and displease Him. A consequence of our sin is suffering. For example, there are many starving children in Africa suffering and dying every day, not as a result of their own sin but as a result of the sin of other nations. Those children suffer from the unequal distribution of wealth, while other children in developed countries often have more than enough food and access to resources than they need. It is unfair, but it was not God who made the world that way. Mankind perverted God's perfection and upset the ways of His immaculate world through disobeying Him.

Paul knew exactly what to say to individuals as well as to the crowds as he witnessed for Christ. He had the opportunity for a one-to-one with the procurator of Judea, Felix. We find out precisely what he focused on during personal evangelism in Acts 24:25: "Now as he reasoned about righteousness, self-control, and the judgment to come, Felix was afraid." The result of Paul's one-on-one was that Felix told him, "Go away for now." Maybe this wasn't Paul's desired result, but at least he couldn't have been found guilty of falsely sweetening the gospel.

A key part of witnessing on a personal and mass scale is also our silent testimony, the way we act. This includes our honesty, humility, kindness, faithfulness, gentleness, and trustworthiness; in other words, all the fruit of the Holy Spirit we produce that others see. Jesus refers to this as letting our light shine out "before men, that they may see your good works and glorify your Father in heaven" in Matthew 5:16. Apart from obedience to Christ and representing our fear of God, our fruit has the express purpose of being a witness of our righteousness for His glory. We must never forget the value of displaying a virtuous character in front of everyone and should always ask God to help us excel in this area. (See the section entitled "Shining Out" in Chapter 11.) According to Deuteronomy 4:6–8, God's law and His Word in our hearts reveal our wisdom and understanding to those around us, which in turn incites admiration from them.

Paul reveals that what is more important to him than his own happiness and comfort is to please others so they might be saved.

> I, too, try to please everyone in everything I do. I don't just do what is best for me; I do what is best for others so that many may be saved.
>
> —1 CORINTHIANS 10:33, NLT

Even when brought before the authorities because of their zeal for spreading the gospel, Peter and John still recognized the seriousness of witnessing. They said, "Do you think God wants us to obey you rather than him? We cannot stop telling about everything we have seen and heard" (Acts 4:19–20, NLT). They did not even fear governmental figures; rather, they overflowed with enthusiasm and commitment to the point of suffering torture because of their dedication to talking about Jesus to others.

Chapter 10

RICHES

Now godliness with contentment is great gain. For we brought nothing into this world, and it is certain we can carry nothing out. And having food and clothing, with these we shall be content. But those who desire to be rich fall into temptation and a snare, and into many foolish and harmful lusts which drown men in destruction and perdition. For the love of money is a root of all kinds of evil, for which some have strayed from the faith in their greediness, and pierced themselves through with many sorrows.

1 Timothy 6:6–10

THE BIBLE CONDEMNS the love of money as being the source of all kinds of evil. Those who chase after great financial or material profit will ultimately fall from the Christian race. Without repentance, they will find themselves in hell. Racing after money and material goods only leads to suffering and humiliation. Instead, we are called to be content with what we have and to thank God for it. Our lives are to center around God, not on treasure here on Earth. Our main concerns should be our riches in Christ Jesus, which is our relationship with God; complete submission to His will; the fact we are now dead to sin and alive in Christ, dependent on Him, obedient to Him, and confident in Him; loving Him and one another; and displaying the fruits and gifts of the Spirit.

This mortal life we have been given is so unstable that our circumstances change all the time. Friends betray us, our money could all be lost in a recession or stolen by thieves, our house could be destroyed by a natural disaster, and our health may go to pot, but God will never fail us. He is the only one in whom we can trust. Not only this, but when the time comes for us to depart from Earth, our money and possessions will be completely useless. They will not save us from death, nor will they help us get into heaven (Luke 12:20–21). For many of us, wealth can in fact be a threat to our salvation (Mark 10:25), so we need to be careful not to be influenced by money. If we find it affects our moods, actions, and attitudes, then its spiritual power is controlling us. When this happens, we are living in the flesh, in disobedience to God.

In fact the Bible tells us riches are worthless (1 Cor. 7:30–31), misleading (Prov. 11:28), fickle (Prov. 23:5), cause greed (Eccles. 5:10), turn us away from God (Mark 4:19), and are not to be desired (Luke 16:25). Regarding Christian leaders and elders, Paul explicitly writes that they must not love money (1 Tim. 3:3).

We are told in 1 John 2:15, 1 John 3:17, and Luke 16:13 that whoever is materialistic and puts a high value on wealth and belongings does not in fact love God. And whoever does not have the love of God in him is not saved. When we seek Him just to get rich, we are on the very wrong path. Rather than material prosperity, the kingdom of heaven is about surrendering to the Lord, which means we have decided we will not control our own destiny but will place it in His hands; dependence on Him; love; righteousness; and defeating evil with good.

In the life of Gehazi, the servant of Elisha, an opportunity to get rich quick arose, and he put God in second place. He used and abused the healing God had done in Naaman for monetary gain, and lied while doing it. In a way he "sold" the work of God. The result was that he and his descendants contracted leprosy (2 Kings 5:27). Gehazi lusted after earthly treasure instead of being satisfied with an eternal reward. The way to measure where the desires of our heart are—whether they are in heaven or on Earth, as in the case of Gehazi—is to assess what we spend most of our time thinking about. Is it God, pleasing Him, and living to treat people as He commanded? Or do we just think about ourselves and our family, our job, the next product or property we want to buy, what we will wear, eat, do, and so forth?

Another warning from Jesus regarding the love of riches is in Matthew 6:19–21: "Don't store up treasures here on earth, where moths eat them and rust destroys them, and where thieves break in and steal. Store your treasures in heaven, where moths and rust cannot destroy…Wherever your treasure is, there the desires of your heart will also be" (NLT). Jesus is basically saying that if the most important thing in our lives is to provide for our own material needs here on Earth, then we are not living to please God but ourselves. When this is the case, God is therefore not the most important element in our lives, which means we cannot be His disciples (Luke 14:26). So if we work to earn money just to feed and satisfy ourselves and our loved ones, spiritually we are dead and do not have our hope in Christ, even if we think we do. At the core of being a true Christian are spiritual, not material matters, and this involves dedicating oneself to His work. Of course, this can be by financially supporting His work as well as by executing it. (See the section entitled "Hard Work" in Chapter 11.)

In Matthew 5:3, Jesus preaches, "God blesses those who are poor and realize their need for him, for the Kingdom of Heaven is theirs" (NLT). Looking closely at this verse, it is clear that Jesus is revealing that it is extremely difficult to be rich and realize one's need for Him. It is much easier to grasp how much we depend on God when we lack material belongings and provisions, as well as basic necessities such as food, water, and access to hygiene, than when we have everything we require. The vast majority of people in the developed world have never been short of such matters, which could be one of the reasons why their churches are much smaller than in some developing countries.

God provides for us materially, yes, but we have to be so careful not to trust in wealth or to place any importance on it.

> Assuredly, I say to you that it is hard for a rich man to enter
> the kingdom of heaven. And again I say to you, it is easier for a

camel to go through the eye of a needle than for a rich man to enter the kingdom of God.

—MATTHEW 19:23–24

Jesus is saying that it is difficult for well-off people to enter heaven because for them it is too easy to fall in love with their possessions and money and rely on them rather than depending on God for everything. The main problem is that the rich easily become selfish people, ignoring the needs of others even though they have more than enough for themselves. Whoever lives this way must give what they have to the poor, and only then can they follow Jesus (Luke 18:22).

The enticement of wealth is a trap every believer should be aware of. Judas Iscariot was so blinded and seduced by monetary gain that he betrayed Jesus. Some Christians do exactly the same thing nowadays. They chose material prosperity over doing the will of God, thereby committing spiritual suicide in the same way that Judas committed physical suicide. Jesus cautions us of this danger in the parable of the sower when He says, "All too quickly the message is crowded out by the worries of this life and the lure of wealth, so no fruit is produced" (Matt. 13:22, NLT). We must always be on guard against the love of money, be content with what we have, trusting God to provide for all our needs.

Most people see material abundance as a sign of God's blessing, but Jesus breaks this paradigm by communicating that it can actually prohibit people from entering heaven, as mentioned above. In fact, those who are rich should boast that God has humbled them, and those who are poor should be proud of their high position (James 1:9–10). This precept points to Matthew 5:5, where Jesus declares that the meek will inherit the earth. Nonetheless, the rich should not be arrogant or place their hope in wealth, but in God alone (1 Tim. 6:17). They must also be generous and full of charitableness (1 Tim. 6:18).

Lavish lifestyles are not a part of God's plan for us either. James 5:5 and Luke 16:19–31 rebuke the rich who spend their resources fattening themselves and on self-indulgence, which include luxuries like expensive clothes, foods, holidays, properties, and material goods. Instead, they should use it to benefit others to the glory of God.

During Amos's time, the Israelites enjoyed prosperity and lived in extravagance. He said to the people:

> You lie on beds inlaid with ivory and lounge on your couches. You dine on choice lambs and fattened calves. You strum away on your harps like David and improvise on musical instruments. You drink wine by the bowlful and use the finest lotions, but you do not grieve over the ruin of Joseph.
>
> —AMOS 6:4–6, NIV

They were too busy seeing to themselves and their own satisfaction to be concerned about God and His people. God says to them in the following verse:

> Therefore you will be among the first to go into exile; your feasting and lounging will end. (NIV)

It is not in vain that the Bible mentions John the Baptist's diet of wild honey and locusts and his camel-hair clothes and leather belt. Such a simple diet and attire show he did not self-indulge. Jesus wasn't even interested in always having the comfort of four walls around Him, as He slept roughly on the Mount of Olives (Luke 21:37). The presence of the Father was His comfort.

What the Bible actually teaches is very different than what we are sometimes led to believe. After Jesus gives instructions concerning not worrying about having enough money, clothes, and food, He instructs us, "Sell your possessions and give to those in need. This will store up treasure for you in heaven!" (Luke 12:33, NLT). Instead of teaching us to keep and enjoy our riches, He tells us to sell them and uses the opportunity to express the need to give and divide what we have with those who don't have enough! When was the last time you heard that preached in church? The early church obeyed this commandment and sold their property and land to distribute the money to the needy (Acts 4:34–35). God's will for us is that we completely and utterly put material interest and the flesh to death.

This was a big concern for Jesus. He became angry and aggressive when He saw people exploiting others and making an inflated profit in God's name. In the temple, which had become more like a marketplace, Jesus showed His vexation, saying, "It is written, My house shall be called the house of prayer; but ye have made it a den of thieves" (Matt. 21:13, KJV). Everyday, worldly life and riches had taken the place of prayer.

We may get angry as we see corrupt political leaders prospering or criminals getting richer and richer, while we may be struggling financially, but we should actually feel sorry for impious people when we see them growing in wealth, because they will soon disappear (Ps. 37:35). It is possible that their riches are what inhibits them from trusting in God and becoming a real Christian. We need to pray that their eyes will be opened, and we must thank God that He has revealed to us the real meaning of life rather than believing in an empty and unfulfilling one.

It is often perversely taught that the apostles were rich and that, therefore, as believers we should also seek financial and material blessing. However, the Bible is very clear that in fact, the apostles were poor. Paul wrote of the apostles, "We are poor, but we give spiritual riches to others. We own nothing yet we have everything" (2 Cor. 6:10, NLT).

Some people use 2 Corinthians 8:9 as an excuse for their greed and materialistic attitudes: "For you know the grace of our Lord Jesus Christ, that though He was rich, yet for your sakes He became poor, that you through His poverty might become rich." The argument is, of course, that the wealth mentioned here is material, not spiritual. If Jesus was materially wealthy, why did the Lord say, "Foxes have holes, and birds of the air have nests; but the Son of man hath not where to lay his head" (Luke 9:58, KJV)? Jesus did not even have His own bed, let alone land or a house! He traveled around from town to town, relying on God for hospitality from people. His concern with belongings was so small that He even told His disciples to not take any money, a bag, extra clothing, sandals, or a walking stick with them when they went out to preach (Matt. 10:9). Jesus shuns those who seek earthly riches at the cost of super-abounding fellowship with God. He made it clear that "a person is a fool to store up earthly wealth but not have a rich relationship with God" (Luke 12:21, NLT).

A very sad fact in many Christian circles today is the presence of the perverse corruption of the word *blessing*. We use this word to mean material as well as spiritual fulfillment, and often it is overused in the material sense. Being blessed refers in the Bible to being poor in spirit, meek, merciful, pure, peacemakers, persecuted, to mourning, and to hungering for righteousness (Matt. 5:3–10). When these things happen to us or we develop these characteristics, only then can we consider ourselves blessed. The next time you use this word, check the context and see if it measures up to Jesus' standard of blessings.

To top it off, Jesus also lamented, "But woe to you who are rich, For you have received your consolation. Woe to you who are full, For you shall hunger" (Luke 6:24–25). Jesus could not have made His teaching clearer on the importance of spiritual prosperity in comparison to material prosperity. Instead of resting our minds on our needs and the tangible goods of the world, we should be seeking God's kingdom above all. Then He will provide for all our concrete needs (Luke 12:31).

Chapter 11

RIGHTEOUS LIVING

The fruit of the righteous is a tree of life.

PROVERBS 11:30, KJV

T HIS PROVERB TELLS us that righteous people produce a tree of life within their own lives. The effect of the tree of life in the Garden of Eden in Genesis 3:22 was perpetual living. Therefore righteous people reap eternal life. Righteousness is the fruit of the work of the Holy Spirit in the Christian, which is produced by union in Jesus (Philippians. 1:11). It actually means being made "right" before God and people (Luke 18:14).

Of course, we are made righteous through our faith in Jesus (Rom. 1:17). When God forgives our sins, He declares us innocent because our debt has been fully paid on the cross by Christ, a perfectly virtuous man who was sacrificed to redeem us. His righteousness is now given to us for free and is called our own by God's grace. We are therefore made upright through Jesus' atoning death on the cross, not by fulfilling any law or set of regulations. Only the Holy Spirit can witness this truth in the hearts of men (John 16:8–10) and therefore declare us innocent. Righteousness by works without faith does not exist. We can never be declared just before God by our own good deeds; only by genuine faith.

While we are made righteous through faith, this same faith will manifest itself in obedience to God's Word, which acts as a moral and practical guide on how to live. Out of love and fear for God, and through the empowering of the Holy Spirit (Rom. 8:3–6), we will naturally live striving to obey everything written in the New Testament.

James points out that faith without righteous deeds is nonexistent (James 2:20). He uses Abraham as an example of righteousness because Abraham obeyed God when he went to sacrifice his most precious possession on the altar, illustrating the unity of faith and action and that one without the other is worthless. This righteousness displayed by Abraham proved his authentic faith, although it didn't save him, for only faith can do that.

In order to define biblical righteousness, I will use Abraham as an example. Abraham's uprightness had varying elements to it:

- his devotion to and fear of God, shown through his willingness to sacrifice Isaac;
- zeal in seeking God (by building many altars to the Lord; see Gen. 12:7–8; 21:33; 13:4, 18);
- his later obedience to God in obeying the Lord's requirements, commands, decrees, and laws (Gen. 26:5);
- his superior knowledge of God by referring to him as "El Olam," translated as "the Eternal God" in Genesis 21:33 (NIV);
- his faith and trust in God ("And he believed in the LORD, and He accounted it to him for righteousness" [Gen. 15:6]);
- his humility when conversing with God about the destruction of Sodom (Gen. 18:27–28);
- his unselfishness in letting Lot choose which land he wanted;
- his refusal to accept worldly wealth from the king of Sodom (Gen. 14:22–24);
- his integrity and generosity in offering a seemingly voluntary tithe to Melchizedek (Gen. 14:20);
- his patience in waiting for God to fulfill His promise (Heb. 6:15);

- his honesty and reliability when he rescued Lot from capture ("So he brought back all the goods, and also brought back his brother Lot and his goods, as well as the women and the people" [Gen. 14:16]).

All these attributes also proved Abraham's faith to be genuine, and therefore he was righteous in God's sight. In the same manner, we should be clothed with all these qualities. We are urged to "put on the new man, which after God is created in righteousness and true holiness" (Eph. 4:24, KJV). We accordingly ought to put off our old way of living and thinking in order to wear like a garment the new creation God has made us into.

Those who have been justified by faith naturally authenticate this work by their righteous and holy living. Righteousness leads to holiness, the profit of which is eternal life (Rom. 6:22). Morality has a pull over us, because we can only be made just if the Holy Spirit is within us. He leads us in morals, teaching us the right and wrong ways to live. Paul uses the terms *slaves to God* and *the control of righteousness* (Rom. 6:20–21, NIV).

Hosea 10:12 compares the work of a farmer to righteousness. As the farmer sows seed in the earth, with time, water, and light a tree with leaves will grow. Then in the right season, juicy fruit matures on it, which serves to nourish people, giving them vitamins and energy. As we, representing the farmers, sow seeds of righteousness and live submissively in order to grow in the faith, seeking God in His word, in prayer, and in fellowship with other believers, then we too will produce delicious fruit. This is the fruit of infallible love, which stretches across political, racial, sexist, and geographical borders as God in turn fills us to the brim and overflowing with His eternal love. Isaiah expresses the fruit of righteousness as a peaceful life (Isa. 32:17).

Living in godliness therefore enables us to walk along the path of life in the peace of God, equipping us for any circumstance, whether good or bad, which might come our way. Our righteousness is not necessarily a ticket to a trouble-free life, but it gives the devil less room to cause havoc and problems for us. In Psalm 22:51, David reveals that because of our hope in God, we will be taken to a place of integrity and uprightness. And because of this, God protects us, not necessarily against temptation, but moreover against temptation overpowering us. Blamelessness also gives us wisdom for coping with every sort of person and shows us how to live (Prov. 11:5).

Job is depicted in the Bible as a righteous person of complete integrity. God said of Job, "There is none like him on the earth, a blameless and upright man, one who fears God and shuns evil" (Job 1:8). On account of this, the devil desired to knock Job over spiritually by accusing him of only showing integrity as a result of God's provisions in his life. Satan wanted to prove that Job was being "paid" for his purity and that deep down inside, Job was really evil because his righteousness was shallow and vain. The devil was questioning God's omniscience in His relationship with a man of integrity. Therefore God permitted the connection between prosperity and saintliness to be broken. Job's trial was this: Did he only trust in God because of what He provides, rather than simply because of who He is? Would Job give up on righteousness when disaster came his way?

How many of us would fall down if God were to test us on the same things? We may find ourselves in a situation similar to Job's one day. Would we pass or fail a test of integrity consisting of despair, loss, physical pain, abandonment, multiple bereavements, loneliness, constant accusation, and God's seeming aloofness?

In this radical test of the genuineness of his righteousness before God and Satan, Job underwent many temptations. His wife encouraged him to curse God (2:9), and the accusations of wrongdoing against him from his former friends did not cease. However, even with God's material provisions uprooted, Job's integrity remained steadfast. He never doubted God's goodness or fairness. He was able to maintain his sincerity and faith, despite losing everything. He persevered in his love and conviction that God is faithful despite His silence and Job's own unjustified suffering.

The key to Job's spiritual success was his genuine fear of and love for God. Job did not trust in the material realm but in the spiritual. He did not complain about the loss of his family and belongings. Rather, he seemed more troubled by God's estrangement from him. He cried out for an explanation of the cause of his distress.

Righteousness is held in high esteem before God. It encompasses our relationship with Him, fear of Him, faith—everything we build our lives around as true Christians. Our enemy recognizes that his best method of attack is to prove us corrupt and godless. Therefore, our best weapon against the devil is our integrity and righteousness.

Righteousness is a part of the armor of God in Ephesians 6 as a weapon against the evil rulers of darkness in the spiritual realms (v. 12). It is our defense before the devil's accusations, giving us power and rights in the spiritual domain. This is because obedience to God's law liberates us from slavery to sin. In light of Job's trial, we must keep upholding integrity always, no matter what the situation is surrounding us.

This includes being a completely trustworthy people so that whatever we say is true and honorable. We ought to steer clear of foolish jokes that serve to trick someone into believing something for our own entertainment, as well as mockery, however light and inoffensive it may seem. We should always think about other people's feelings first and foremost and put ourselves in their place, constantly asking ourselves, How would I want them to treat me? (Matt. 7:12).

Psalm 15:3 states that to see God and know His presence, we should practice no evil against others. This means we must be careful not to harbor hatred, anger, jealousy, pride, greed, bitterness, negativity (including gossip), feelings of rejection, and vengeance. These elements do us more harm than our neighbor because they put a wedge between us and God. Allowing any of these feelings to brew within us makes our soul sick (Prov. 18:7; Ps. 6:3; 19:7) and can cause other problems, such as insomnia, headaches, depression, sicknesses, anguish, fear, exhaustion, anxiety, and stress. In order to be free of these tribulations and for the healing of our soul, we must walk blamelessly and do what is righteous.

Characteristics like "anger, wrath, malice, blasphemy, filthy language" (Col. 3:8), as well as "all bitterness, wrath, anger, clamor, and evil speaking" (Eph. 4:31), should be completely foreign and no longer a part of our everyday living. They simply cannot dwell in the life of a believer. If they do, that person is not walking in the Spirit but living in disobedience to God.

Ananias and Sapphira from Acts 5 lacked moral integrity in their attempts to deceive God and the believers. They wanted to be known as honorable and perhaps desired to exalt themselves before the apostles by pretending to sacrifice all the money they received from selling their piece of land, whereas in fact they kept some for themselves. This pricey deceit and hypocrisy cost them their lives, as God immediately struck them dead in the presence of Peter and other believers. This is a stern warning for us when we are tempted to be dishonest.

Honesty is so important for Christians that Jesus orders us to "just say a simple, 'Yes, I will,' or 'No, I won't.' Anything beyond this is from the evil one" (Matt. 5:37, NLT). Here, Jesus is instructing the people not to use certain expressions in order to validate or invalidate their promises. We shouldn't need to have a special word to support the fact that we are telling the truth or that our word will be fulfilled; we should be so full of integrity and trustworthiness that just a yes or no on its own will suffice.

James believed that a large part of righteous behavior is looking after the poor and needy, helping the oppressed and those without family (James 1:27), as well as keeping free from worldly pollution. Peter summed it up neatly by saying, "Turn away from evil and do good…seek peace and pursue it" (1 Pet. 3:11).

It is God who gives us the ability to walk in rectitude, and He gives us the harvest of righteousness. We are unable to manage anything by our own effort alone. There needs to be effort on our part, together with God's work in our lives, in order for us to live righteously (2 Cor. 9:10–11).

GODLINESS

> And the Lord—who is the Spirit—makes us more and more like
> him as we are changed into his glorious image.
> —2 CORINTHIANS 3:18, NLT

Our goal in life is to become more and more like Christ; we are to imitate Him. Obviously He is God and we are not. We are made in His image only and are limited by and subject to His will. Children are never greater than their fathers, and in the same way we are not as great as God but are subordinate to Him. Imitating Christ means acting in the same manner He acted and lived, in reverent obedience to God here on Earth, and in purity, loving and accepting everyone, no matter what their social standing is. Jesus' outlook on life must be ours. Everything He did, He did because He saw the Father doing it. He did nothing of His own will (John 5:19). He had complete unity and was totally submitted to His Father. Nothing He said or did was of His own accord.

Christlikeness is remaining faithful and obedient to the Lord's teachings and truth. Then, "the truth will set you free" (John 8:32, NIV), meaning that through godliness and obedience to God, we have freedom from oppression of the devil and sin. We are no longer slaves but free sons of God.

Godliness is a way of behavior and a specific mentality, in the same way the Victorians had a certain type of conduct and thought process they conformed to, for example. The biblical definition of *godliness* is:

- carrying out God's will—"He listens to the godly man who does his will" (John 9:31, NIV).
- living self-controlled and upright lives as we wait in hope for Jesus' return (Titus 2:11–13)
- clothing ourselves with Jesus (Rom. 13:14)
- an instinctive characteristic of a close relationship with God—"Noah was a righteous man, the only blameless man living on earth at the time. He consistently followed God's will and enjoyed a close relationship with him" (Gen. 6:9, NLT 1996).

The Holy Spirit is our primary aide and strength to become godly, but we must allow Him to work within us and obey His calling. It is not the Holy Spirit on His own who works out a godly life within us; there is a balance between relying on His working and our own exertion. For example, there are admonitions in the New Testament regarding saintliness. One is in 1 Timothy 4:7–8, where we are told, "Train yourself to be godly. For physical training is of some value, but godliness has value for all things, holding promise for both the present life and the life to come" (NIV). Paul is demonstrating that godliness requires self-discipline and self-control in the same way an athlete who trains for a race also sacrifices himself to perform to the best of his ability. We must strive (Philippians 3:12) every day to conform ourselves to the godly nature along with the help, motivation, and strength of the Holy Spirit.

Another admonition is to cast "down arguments and every high thing that exalts itself against the knowledge of God, bringing every thought into captivity to the obedience of Christ" (2 Cor. 10:5). Paul does not say that God takes captive our every thought to make it obedient to Himself; rather, we do. Godliness deals with every single area of our lives and causes us to renounce absolutely everything that doesn't reflect Christ. This can include clever, nice-sounding, and logical theology, however unbiblical; the music we listen to; our passions, habits, cravings, and fears; unprofitable time-spending; pride and boastfulness.

Being godly is not something that occurs instantly, but instead it takes time to develop. As God works out our salvation within us, godliness starts to manifest itself in different forms—through our attitudes, in our thoughts, in our actions, in our outlook on life, in our plans for the future, our daily and long-term desires, in how we treat other people, in how we spend our time, and in what we speak. Godliness goes hand in hand with spiritual wisdom. As we grow in intimacy and knowledge of God, our reaction to understanding who He is and His wonderful love and mercy leads us to instinctively become more Christlike. Also, through our growing knowledge of Him, all our spiritual needs are met to live a life of purity and holiness (2 Pet. 1:3).

One reason to keep moving forward to become godly is that it gives us meaning and a reason to live now, and also everything we do that reflects God and our faith in Jesus will remain standing and have its results in the next life (1 Tim. 4:8). When we waste time and behave as if we have never been enlightened by God's truth, then that is not living with an eternal perspective. Instead, it is saying that we are living for this life and are not thinking about the next. We need to understand that what we do in this life reflects on the life to come. Second Corinthians 4:17 tells us that "our light affliction, which is but for a moment, is working for us a far more exceeding and eternal weight of glory." Our eternal reward gives us all the more reason to press on and, despite our suffering in this world, imitate Christ in every area of our lives.

A result of being godly in the world, especially among unbelieving company, is that we will be hated (Luke 21:17) and persecuted (2 Tim. 3:12). However, our reward far outweighs the cost: "But not a hair of your head will perish! By standing firm, you will win your souls" (Luke 21:18–19, NLT).

Part of leading a life of godliness is always being prepared in every situation to give a testimony about God's work in our life (Col. 4:5–6). Wherever we go and whatever we do, we must represent the light and shine out so people see we are different. We must always go everywhere with a missionary purpose.

SHINING OUT

> You are the light of the world. A city on a hill cannot be hidden. Neither do people light a lamp and put it under a bowl. Instead they put it on its stand, and it gives light to everyone in the house. In the same way, let your light shine before men, that they may see your good deeds and praise your Father in heaven.
> —MATTHEW 5:14–16, NIV

As Christians in a dark world, our radiance must glow forth as we stick out. The church must not hide its luminosity. We were taken out of the darkness and shown the light of Christ so men would be able to see the difference in us in order for us to illuminate their lives. God calls us to shine our light in the whole house, not in just one corner or one room. This means that we must be characterized by God's luminous energy as Christ shines His light on us.

We will shine brightly in this way when we really and truly find satisfaction in God. The only way to arrive at this point is to completely give up the lusts and desires of the flesh, vainglory, and the aspiration to control our own lives. When we are entirely surrendered to Him, we will feel whole and satisfied spiritually because of the righteousness He gives us (Matt. 5:6). The Beatitudes are not commandments; rather, they are observations on what the Christian life is supposed to be like.

Each one of us has a collective commitment within the church to be light to all those there, but we also have a personal commitment to be radiant in our private lives, before our friends and family members.

Our light is characterized by our fruit, which is produced in "goodness and righteousness and truth" (Eph. 5:9, KJV). As people see Jesus within us through the holy living we have been called to, people will be drawn to the gospel in the same way that bugs are attracted to light. This means we are, in fact, ushering in the coming of His kingdom (2 Pet. 3:9, 11–12). As our light shines on them, not only does it convict and expose their sin (Eph. 5:11), but it also helps them along the way to come to a revelation of God's love.

Without light, everything stops. At night, most people do not work because the majority of businesses and commerce halt. In the same way, the people of the world, even though they don't know it, are in spiritual darkness and have absolutely no hope unless they see our light. We must allow them to see it in order for them to have a chance of knowing the truth. Jesus left us warnings about covering up our light before the world. He gives three places in the Gospel of Luke where that light shouldn't be found:

- *Under a bowl* (Luke 11:33, NIV). Bowls are used to eat out of, representing the desires of the flesh. When our flesh starts winning the spiritual battle and we give in to its wants, then we start to do what pleases it and not what our spirit desires. When we are in this state, our light is no longer visible to those around us; it is covered up by our evil and fleshly attitudes, thoughts, and actions.
- *Under the bed* (Luke 8:16). The bedroom, an intimate place, is a place of secrets where people sleep, and no one apart from the person or couple who sleep there knows what goes on

inside. This could represent the hidden sins in our heart that conceal our light, the sins that happen in our thought-life that only God sees. There should be no separation between God and the deepest parts within our soul. We should open our heart to Him in such a way that we try to hide nothing (John 3:21). Adam attempted to conceal himself from God behind a tree because of the guilt of his sin. Only when the Lord called him did he admit his transgression. We must always confess our sins before God, or we will find our light losing its brightness. (See the section entitled "Confession of Sin" in Chapter 11.)

- *Under a jar or vessel* (Luke 8:16, NIV, KJV). These are both containers for mundane foodstuffs or household items, representing the busyness of daily life—not necessarily evil desires—that crowd out God's truth in us. Martha fell into this trap when she was more concerned about preparing dinner than she was about spiritual matters (Luke 10:38–42). This has a habit of manifesting in us in the form of inventing excuses to not go to church, pray, read the Bible, be honest, or work out our salvation. Instead, we waste time on neutral activities. When we start justifying not feeding our soul in this way, the lack of spiritual food prevents people from seeing Jesus in our lives. We cloud out what makes us shine with laziness as we start to backslide. The invitees in the parable of the banquet came up with excuses, and because of that they were not allowed to attend the banquet. We need to make sure our pretenses are not blocking our light or we will find ourselves with the same destination as those first invited to the feast of the kingdom of God. This also begs the question, How many talents are hidden inside us under excuses? (See the section entitled "Hard Work" in Chapter 11.)

It is essential that our light be not covered up by anything, especially pretexts, sins, and unspiritual desires. Instead, as we shake off these hindrances and seek God in the beauty of holiness, we must seize every opportunity to shine out for Christ through speaking the truth, through our deeds, and through silent witness because we are urged to "make the most of every opportunity" in these dark days (Eph. 5:16, NLT). A lamp is more effective in darkness than when it shines in the presence of other lamps, because in the dark it dispels the blackness. But in the light, there is no blackness to dissipate. This analogy signifies that when we shine out among the spiritually dead, although the battle is harder, the victory is greater, and it brings more glory to Christ.

Apart from God using our light to speak to others, whether Christians or not, about who He is and His love, we also use our light to fight battles in the spiritual realm. The way to put on our "armour of light" (Rom. 13:12, KJV) is through overcoming evil with good. For example, when an evil thought pops into our mind about someone who has trespassed against us, instead of dwelling on it and desiring trouble to happen to that person, we must immediately turn away from the evil thought and instead bless them and pray for them.

Vengeance and Defense

> Dear friends, never take revenge. Leave that to the righteous anger of God. For the Scriptures say, "I will take revenge; I will pay them back," says the Lord.
> —Romans 12:19, NLT

God, who is omniscient, omnipresent, and omnipotent, is man's ultimate Judge. When we have done no wrong, He is our great Defender and Avenger against unfounded accusations and wrongdoing, because He knows every hidden thought and secret, something impossible for any man or earthly judge. He decided what was right and wrong even before the world began. There is not an ounce of corruption or biased favor in Him when it comes to taking revenge and defending the weak and indefensible. For any unfairness we patiently endure on Earth, God will reveal who is right and who is wrong on Judgment Day and will deal with each party accordingly (2 Cor. 5:10).

Before then, when we trust God to defend and repay us rather than defending and seeking vengeance ourselves before our earthly enemies, we will find evenhandedness come our way when we are innocent. God is compassionate and concerned with giving justice to the humble. The psalmists sometimes questioned God as to why He could seemingly take His time in doing this (Ps. 13:1; 88:14), but they never doubted His willingness and capability to act on their behalves. Jesus' silent submission to baseless allegations and abuse is portrayed in 1 Peter 2:23: "When they hurled their insults at him, he did not retaliate; when he suffered, he made no threats. Instead, he entrusted himself to him who judges justly" (NIV). He left His defense completely in the hands of God.

Jesus teaches this subservient and defenseless attitude in Matthew 5:39–40:

> But I tell you not to resist an evil person. But whoever slaps you on your right cheek, turn the other to him also. If anyone wants to sue you and take away your tunic, let him have your cloak also.

Whenever we are mistreated, we must always place the situation in God's hands and trust Him. We must humble ourselves before our attacker and bless them. If we take the situation in our own hands and avenge our injustice, we will be sinning against God for not depending on Him and for displaying pride. Even if it seems like God is not doing anything, we have to rest in His just character and remember that patience is necessary as we wait for His advocacy, either in this life or the next.

> Say not thou, I will recompense evil; but wait on the LORD, and he shall save thee.
> —PROVERBS 20:22, KJV

When accusations against us are directly related to our evangelism and what we believe regarding the gospel of Jesus Christ (i.e., they are against God rather than us personally), Jesus gives His word that the Holy Spirit will teach us what to say in defense (Luke 12:11–12). We read throughout Acts that the apostle Paul defended himself in court many times and also before the mob in Jerusalem (Acts 22). When Jesus was slandered by the religious Jews and Pharisees, He often gave short defenses in order to teach them the right way (Mark 2:17; John 18:23). Sometimes He phrased this in the form of a challenging question (Luke 6:9; Mark 2:8–10).

For us, posing a challenging question in defense of the gospel needs to be carefully thought through, as these questions can sometimes be wrongly used to get back at the person or institution out of spite or to display anger or revenge. They ought to be utilized for the good of the receiving party, to cut to the true issue and explore the subliminal, making the receiver think deeper about the topic. A perfect example of challenging questions is when Jesus asked the Jews in John 8:46, "Which of you can truthfully accuse me of sin? And since I am telling you the truth, why don't you believe me?" (NLT). He went straight to the heart of the matter within the questions—the Jews' lack of right to accuse Him and their unbelief. We need to be wise before forming the question so as to make sure no prejudice is hidden and there are no suppositions made about the other person's beliefs or life. Also, Jesus possibly did not seem to expect an answer to these questions, and neither should we.

Apart from cases in which Christianity is being put on the line, sticking up for our innocence against unfounded lies will be of no benefit anyway. Accusers are often biased and have normally already made up their minds about us; therefore, they will not even listen to our cases. We will just frustrate ourselves by arguing with a brick wall. Humility is the key to keeping quiet and trusting in and waiting for God.

DONATING

> Assuredly, I say to you that this poor widow has put in more than all those who have given to the treasury; for they all put in out of their abundance, but she out of her poverty put in all that she had, her whole livelihood.
>
> —MARK 12:43–44

When God's love fills our hearts, we naturally feel charitable toward one another. As we freely give to others, we should feel buoyant and extremely happy. This is interlinked with an alleviating feeling that we are not tied down to our earthly possessions but have been set free from slavery to them and from placing any importance on them. In Jesus' words, "It is more blessed to give than to receive" (Acts 20:35, KJV), meaning that the giver actually profits from his contribution more than the receiver! Philanthropy also acts as a sacrifice of praise to the Lord as we demonstrate love for the mankind He created.

The quantity of money or goods we decide to donate is not of primary importance to God. What is significant is to give with a sincere heart before Him, not with ulterior motives like pride, seeking the praise of men, and not giving it grudgingly or in response to pressure from man (2 Cor. 9:5–7). We should contribute with gladness and trust in God that He will use our sacrifices for His glory. When the Macedonian Christians gave to Christ's witnesses in Jerusalem, they "gave themselves first to the Lord" (2 Cor. 8:5, NIV). This is the key to all Christian giving, to present ourselves to God and give as if dedicating our gift to Him, wholly and with no reservations.

The widow mentioned in Mark 12:43–44, quoted at the beginning of this section, is proof enough that the quantity we donate is only important compared to the total wealth and income we have (2 Cor. 8:12). The poor widow gave everything she had. Even though it was not a lot in monetary terms, it was priceless to God. In the same way, Christ gave up everything He had for us. He forsook all His glory to serve us and lay down His life for our sakes. We are called to give as much as we can, mirroring this. With this in focus, we should never judge donations by quantities; rather, we should leave that to God, because only He knows how much everyone gives in relation to their resources. Some churches honor people who give larger quantities of money over those who give less; this is unbiblical and looking at things from a human point of view rather than God's.

We also need to be careful not to allow ourselves to be bullied into making a contribution by men and churches. Some churches will even do this using Bible verses, gentle speech, and good manners. Instead, we should be checking the states of our hearts before the Lord and making sure we present our gifts to Him freely, generously, wholeheartedly, and joyfully. What we give is only acceptable if given "eagerly" (2 Cor. 8:12, NLT).

Throughout the whole of the Bible, God demonstrates a deep concern and care for the needs of the poor. This is central to His character. All throughout the Mosaic Law it is made evident (Deut. 24:19–21), and Jesus came to Earth to preach "the gospel to the poor" (Luke 4:18). In turn, the Lord urges His people to do the same.

> If anyone has material possessions and sees his brother in need
> but has no pity on him, how can the love of God be in him?
>   —1 JOHN 3:17, NIV

Part of the Christian character should be generosity toward and regard for the poor (Ps. 112:9). John the Baptist preached that for the person who truly repents, their fruit will display itself as they share their means with those in need. He taught, "He answereth and saith unto them, He that hath two coats, let him impart to him that hath none; and he that hath meat, let him do likewise" (Luke 3:11, KJV).

The act of giving generously is actually a gift of the Spirit (Rom. 12:8) and a ministry within the body of Christ (2 Cor. 9:13). One is supposed to "give to him who asks you, and from him who wants to borrow from you do not turn away" (Matt. 5:42). This involves making sure we have provisions on hand for those who plead and getting into the habit of accepting requests rather than turning them down.

Unfortunately, some have seen the Christian doctrine of giving as an easy open door to become rich and make the most out of honest people's obedience to God's Word. This is why it is important to prayerfully decide which causes and ministries we will financially support. Paul did everything he possibly could to avoid criticism and prove his and Titus's transparency with the gift from the Corinthian church (2 Cor. 8:20–21). This means that ministries and organizations that collect money must be open and careful with offerings, and we should be cautious about donating to charities and institutions who decide they are unable to be economically candid and incapable of revealing their financial data. Even if we do donate to such establishments cheerfully and as an act of worship to God, we will still be rewarded. They are answerable to God for what they do with our offerings, not us as the giver if we give in ignorance to their dishonesty.

The result of true Christian giving is receiving in return God's abundant grace, enabling us to walk in righteousness and holiness (2 Cor. 9:6–8). The receiver's needs are met, and he or she will feel inspired to offer thanksgiving and praise to God and prayer for the givers (2 Cor. 9:12–14). Jesus inspires beneficence, and the consequence is receiving God's blessings in return (Luke 6:38).

HARD WORK

> Never be lazy, but work hard and serve the Lord enthusiastically.
>
> —ROMANS 12:11, NLT

Throughout the Bible, hard work is held in high esteem. Genesis begins with a description of God's creative activity, which lasted six days. Because of His satisfaction with it, He "rested from all his work" (Gen. 2:2, NLT). The Book of Revelation ends with God's declaration of His labor, "I am making everything new!" (Rev. 21:5, NIV). God's creative production is a wonderful illustration of His persistent exertion and also His faithful providence for His people. Jesus divulges that the Father does not stop working (John 5:17). In the same way, we too should not stop doing good. When we become Christians, our calling is to do God's work. He becomes our Boss, and we have a responsibility to represent His love and compassion to all people.

When Jesus was made incarnate, He came to do God's will and "finish His work" (John 4:34). We need to make an effort to do the same. There is always work to do for God. Jesus informs us there will always be poor among us, and He left us the Great Commission to preach the news of God's saving grace. (See Chapter 9, "Evangelizing," and the section entitled "Faith with Works" in Chapter 3.) This is the most important type of work we can do, because it involves being totally dedicated to Him and advancing His kingdom.

Instead of working to earn money to feed ourselves and our families, Jesus says, "Labour not for the meat which perisheth, but for that meat which endureth unto everlasting life, which the Son of man shall give unto you: for him hath God the Father sealed" (John 6:27, KJV). Of course, everyone needs to earn money to eat and survive in this world, but Jesus is saying not to spend all our energy on earning to fill ourselves with material food and pleasures. We need to be involved in spiritual work as well—in our churches, in our neighborhoods, in our jobs, in our towns and cities, wherever we feel God's call. This is to be done practically, helping people with their problems, whether it be offering advice and support or meeting their material and spiritual needs, interceding and lifting up people in prayer.

Jesus warned of ignoring the importance of carrying out His Father's work in the parable of the talents. In this story, two out of the three servants invested the talents they had been given and got good returns. However, the third servant did not invest his talents and hence did not make a profit. To sum up the meaning of the parable, Jesus says, "To those who use well what they are given, even more will be given, and they will have an abundance. But from those who do nothing, even what little they have will be taken away. Now throw this useless servant into outer darkness, where there will be weeping and gnashing of teeth'" (Matt. 25:29–30, NLT). This serves as a warning to us. If we are not actively seeking how to use the gifts and finances that God has given us to glorify Him and advance His kingdom, we may be surprised with the outcome on Judgment Day. We need to keenly search where we can do works that cost us either time, money, or effort—works we are not gaining fair earthly payment for.

The Bible gives us examples of where we can use the talents we have been given.

> In his grace, God has given us different gifts for doing certain things well. So if God has given you the ability to prophesy, speak out with as much faith as God has given you. If your gift is serving others, serve them well. If you are a teacher, teach well.

If your gift is to encourage others, be encouraging. If it is giving, give generously. If God has given you leadership ability, take the responsibility seriously. And if you have a gift for showing kindness to others, do it gladly.

—ROMANS 12:6–8, NLT

Diligence in the Scriptures not only refers to earnestness in seeking God and carrying out His work but likewise to the attitude we should have in our worldly jobs, which sustain us materially. This should be honorable work with nothing questionable about it (Titus 3:14), done with integrity and honesty. As a result of the idleness amongst some in the Thessalonian church, Paul felt he had to set a rule among them that whoever did not earn money could not eat (2 Thess. 3:10). He wanted them to learn the importance of responsibility and conscientiousness in order to be able to share with the needy (Eph. 4:28; Acts 20:35), so that they would not live dependent on others (1 Thess. 4:12) as a people with empty lives (Titus 3:14).

Paul is a prime example of hard work (1 Thess. 2:9). He labored with perseverance for the gospel, but in addition to his faithfulness and vigor in this area, he consciously decided not to live off offerings and handouts from the Thessalonians. Instead, he chose to sustain himself as a tentmaker. Could you imagine the image of some ministries today if, instead of relying on donations, they supported themselves? Paul was afraid of giving reason for anyone to weaken in the faith as a result of possible suspicions that he was cashing in on his ministry, and he wanted to make sure the Thessalonians wouldn't feel bogged down by his extra financial weight. This gave another reason for God to be glorified among them. Paul practiced what he preached, as he set a good example for those who had lost the habit of honest hard work. (Although, of course, it is perfectly biblical to live off God's work. See 1 Timothy 5:18.)

This spiritual work mentioned above includes working at our relationship with God. We should strive for and spend most of our efforts seeking Him with all our heart (Jer. 29:13). This is the most important work we can do because Christianity is about a relationship with God. In second place is relating to people, so we must be vigilant against the ministry becoming our god in place of the Lord God. As part of working on our bond with Him, we must similarly strive after Christlikeness (2 Pet. 1:5–8). Jesus instigates us to "work hard to enter the narrow door to God's Kingdom, for many will try to enter but will fail. When the master of the house has locked the door, it will be too late" (Luke 13:24–25, NLT).

In Proverbs, laziness is condemned as disgraceful, a danger, and the cause of poverty (Prov. 10:5, 26; 24:33–34). Paul offers a word of caution regarding idleness. There is a danger of becoming a busybody and a gossip (2 Thess. 3:12). This causes divisions and arguments within churches, sowing cruelness, negativity, and causing accusations. Paul recommends keeping away from such people in the body of Christ (2 Thess. 3:6) and warning them of their sin (v. 15).

There is just one more problem with spiritual lethargy—how infectious it is and how easy it is to practice. After all, no effort is involved! All it takes is being enticed by sleep and rest, "and poverty will come on you like a bandit" (Prov. 24:34, NIV). When we start making excuses not to pray, seek God, and obey Him—just as the sluggard defends not working because of the dangers of going out into the street (Prov. 26:13)—it means we are falling prey to slothfulness. We must remember our calling (Rom. 12:11) and ponder how quickly this life passes by, recalling Paul's example and his focus on the eternal reward.

CONFESSION OF SIN

> If we confess our sins, he is faithful and just to forgive us our sins, and to cleanse us from all unrighteousness.
>
> —1 JOHN 1:9, KJV

The confession of sin is declaring our own transgressions and guilt to God or another believer (James 5:16). Sin can produce in us a heavy and oppressive spiritual burden (Ps. 38:4). This can eat away at our guilt, consciences, and spiritual lives, making us weary without realizing it (Ps. 73:21–22). When we sin, it makes our souls ill. It takes away our peace, which we so desperately need, and it interrupts our fellowship with God. Ultimately, it causes death (Rom. 5:12).

As we confess our sins, we can sometimes feel the weight of the burden being lifted off us, and through forgiveness we will be restored to our relationship with Christ. This is a spiritual victory. According to 1 John 1:9, confession purifies us from unrighteousness and therefore takes us to a righteous state before an upright God. Our souls are then healed (Ps. 41:4).

David reveals in Psalm 32 the freedom granted our soul when we admit our sins to the Lord. It also shows what happens when we do not acknowledge our sins. David could not feel peace; he just groaned all day long (v. 3), and his mind was deeply troubled. If we hide our sins from God and do not come out with them in the open, the sin trapped within will cause us to suffer psychologically and sometimes physically (Ps. 38:3). He refers to those who are not honest enough to confess their sins to God as those whose spirit is deceived. Only when we acknowledge our sin will we find ourselves free of guilt and greatly relieved (v. 5). David tells us that whoever's sin is forgiven, that man is blessed (v. 2).

However, confession is never as easy as it sounds. There are many spiritual and intellectual barriers that prevent us from confessing what's destroying our souls.

Firstly, we may believe confession is out of date and therefore irrelevant. It is rarely preached in churches nowadays, and the image it conjures is often that of a confession box in a Catholic church. However, to rediscover its potential, we need look no further than the Book of James: "Therefore confess your sins to each other and pray for each other so that you may be healed" (James 5:16, NIV). Exposing our sin to other respected Christians whom we know are spiritually mature and trustworthy does wonders to free the soul from bondage. It can also symbolize genuine repentance. A time of prayer should follow a session of admitting guilt, since God is the one who ultimately forgives us. We need to always turn to Him.

Secondly, our own egos can come between us and confession. It can be embarrassing revealing what we shouldn't have done in front of God or another person, so a step of faith and humility are necessary. Fear also acts as a stumbling block and a pretext not to do it. We shouldn't worry about reactions to our confessed sin, nor should we search for a reaction from the person to whom we confess. Sometimes prior worrying about this becomes a stronghold in our minds. The more we think about confessing, the more absurd it seems, so its effectiveness becomes warped. We must trust God's love and mercy and just do it in obedience to His Word. We must take courage to overcome any fear of confession. We need this healing for our souls, so we must be strong and mature to make the decision to come clean.

Thirdly, the devil tells us the sin we need to acknowledge was not actually a sin at all and that therefore the acknowledgment of guilt is not necessary. Sin distances us from God, and as we find ourselves falling further and further away from Him, His high standard of holiness is lowered in our minds. When this happens, we start accepting sins as "half-sins" or as something God isn't bothered about. This attitude comes from the world, as society is accepting more and more lewd behavior as normal and even honorable. When we feel ourselves backsliding in this way, our alarm bells need to ring and we should kneel before God in a humble state of confession, asking for His forgiveness.

Proverbs 28:13 tells us, "He who conceals his sins does not prosper, but whoever confesses and renounces them finds mercy" (NIV). Confession opens our eyes to God's love and mercy and fills us with peace and inner joy. It restores our relationship with Him, so we need to boldly get close to the throne of grace and confess to the Lord, overcoming any impediment in His authority. We will then be covered by His divine mercy. This quote in Proverbs is very important because it reminds us that declaration of guilt on its own isn't enough. We need to actually turn away from the sin. We must give up everything that distances us from God and displeases Him to enable us to grow in love, knowledge, and purity.

After receiving forgiveness from God, we must forget our sin and give ourselves completely over to Him. God will then restore us to the honored status of being His dearly beloved children (Eph. 5:1–5). Just looking back on sin with pleasure and happiness is a sin itself. We have been born again into a new life, so we must turn our backs on the mistakes committed in the past and not live relishing in the old times. After confessing, forget the past and move on. Try and recall only the good memories, not the bad ones. And if you can't forget, do not dwell on them. Make every effort to put them to the back of your mind.

Sometimes the confession of sins committed before we became a Christian is preached in church. This involves digging out the past to clean it up, psychiatric methods of mental healing, and sometimes even hypnosis. This process is often referred to as "internal healing," and it is taught that opening old mental and spiritual wounds and confessing them has some value. However, this egotistical doctrine blatantly contradicts the power of the cross, which affirms that faith in Christ means we are forgiven of our past. It's saying that faith in the cross of Jesus isn't sufficient to be set free. It subtly teaches that through Jesus' sacrifice we have a new life but that it is not enough; we also have to recall and denounce past influences, mistakes, problems, involvement in other religions and practices, vices, sicknesses, genetic problems, and ancestral curses to really be free in Christ. What biblical basis does this have? None. We have been made new creations, born into a new life (2 Cor. 5:17), and Jesus has wonderfully wiped our slates clean from our former mistakes.

This deception was designed to take our focus away from our relationship with God and from loving Him and one another in order to become engrossed in ourselves. It is based on heathen science and needs to be avoided, because Paul tells us to leave the past behind (Philippians 3:13). This is quite an amazing instruction from someone who prior to becoming a Christian was violently involved in persecuting the church. We may also look to the example of the parable of the lost son. When the lost son had returned to his father's house and started confessing his sin to his father, the father interrupted him and didn't even let him finish his speech (Luke 15:20–24)!

The answer to every spiritual problem Christians suffer from can be found in the Bible, by studying it and seeking God. A self-help course other than a completely biblical one is not needed. God is everything we require

(Gen. 18:14; Job 42:2). John 8:31–32 tells us that the answer to freedom from our past is in believing in Jesus and obeying His teachings.

THANKSGIVING

What I want instead is your true thanks to God.
—PSALM 50:14, NLT 1996

It is of utmost importance to always remember to show our appreciation to God for everything. We need to recognize that everything we have comes from Him—our lives, our health, the health of our families, our accommodations, our friends and families, our belongings, our churches, our towns, our acquaintances, our livelihoods, our spiritual battles and victories, our spiritual giftings and fruit, the Bible, the love and sacrifice of Jesus, eternal life. For everything that we have, whether physical, spiritual, or material, we must always have a thankful heart before God. Our thanksgiving should be incorporated into our daily prayers, coming from sincerity. It is supposed to be a part of our daily communion with God, in the same way that His provisions are daily (Matt. 6:11).

Even in times of trouble, if we thank God, we will be proving to Him that we are truly submissive and genuinely His children. Paul tells the Thessalonians, "In everything give thanks; for this is the will of God in Christ Jesus for you" (1 Thess. 5:18). This also strengthens our faith in times of testing and difficulty. David, pleading with God for protection from his enemies and for his very his life in Psalm 35, still praised Him for His righteousness in verse 28 and pledged to thank Him publicly in verse 18. This radical submission to God, in which we express gratitude to Him and recognize His goodness in whatever the circumstance, should be every Christian's goal. It is the type of triumphant attitude that leads to victory.

Jesus revolutionized thanksgiving. He thanked God by faith. That is to say, before He saw the Lord's intervention, He thanked Him for the result. Before Lazarus had risen from the dead, Jesus thanked His Father for the miracle about to happen (John 11:41). Jesus also thanked God for the broken bread and wine poured out before He sacrificed His body on the cross.

Whatever we are believing God for in prayer, we should also be overflowing with gratitude toward Him for the unseen outcome.

One area where Jesus never failed to offer a prayer of gratitude to God was before eating. He always blessed the food and thanked God for it (Matt. 15:36; Luke 22:17). As our perfect model, we should bless and honor God for our nutriment too, not in a religious or ceremonious way, but from a heart truly grateful for God's provision.

In order to be genuinely appreciative for the food we eat, we need to really believe and recognize that it is God who has given it to us. It is not by our own efforts we have it. We do not have enough to eat because we had a good upbringing, for example, and therefore have never involuntarily suffered from hunger. Nor does our sustenance come from our monthly paychecks, nor from our spouses' or parents' provision. Rather, we have a full plate of food before us because of God's goodness toward us. He loves us with unfailing love and cares for all our needs. It comes from God, who, in His grace, lets us have enough to eat and replenishes our body with the nutrients and goodness it needs to be sustained.

As God created us with His own hands, He designed our bodies in such a way that they require water and food. He gave us a perfect digestive system and with it gave us pleasure in eating. At first He gave us seed-bearing plants to consume (Gen. 1:29), and after the flood He allowed and capacitated us to have meat (Gen. 9:3). If we keep this perspective in mind, we should find ourselves truly grateful every time before eating.

In addition to this, we should be thankful for the spiritual provisions He affords us. This includes giving thanks for His Word and the revelation of it, the lessons He personally gives us throughout the race of life, and what He has done for us personally and generally, for the freedom from sin and death we have been given in Christ (Ps. 30:11–12). Always feeling indebted to God regarding these elements will help us to never forget all the good He has done and remember where we have come from; spiritual ignorance. It also reminds us of His nearness and that He is a personal God who wants to be involved in our lives.

Through recognizing His blessings, we gain strength from Him to be triumphant in every situation. Daniel thanked God for the wisdom and power he was given (Dan. 2:23), and Paul was always careful to acknowledge God for other people's spiritual blessings, such as their faith (Rom. 1:8), love (2 Thess. 1:3), obedience (Rom. 6:17), and enthusiasm (2 Cor. 8:16). Both Daniel and Paul were victorious in their walk with God; they remained firm until the end.

As a part of our regular adoration of and relationship with God, we must also ceaselessly remember to thank Him for who He is, for the eternal nature of His love (2 Chron. 20:21), His goodness (1 Chron. 16:34), His righteousness (Ps. 7:17), for His strength and protection (Ps. 28:7), His wonderful deeds (Ps. 75:1), His creativity (Ps. 100:1–3), His kingdom (Heb. 12:48), His greatness (Ps. 95:2–5), His salvation (Ps. 106:47), for being a personal God (Ps. 118:28), for His name (Ps. 100:4), His comfort and compassion (Is. 51:3), His mercy (Jer. 30:18–19), for rescuing us (Ps. 116:17), for being our source of strength (1 Tim. 1:12), for His grace (1 Cor. 1:4), His peacefulness (Col. 3:15), His wisdom (Job 12:13), His power (Rev. 11:17), His holiness (Ps. 30:4), and for answering prayers (Ps. 118:21), amongst many others. Such responsiveness to God's attributes is a natural reaction as we reflect on Him, get to know Him better, and become smaller as He becomes greater in our lives.

In addition to this, it is important to keep in mind the value of showing gratitude to one another as brothers and sisters in Christ (1 Cor. 16:18). Paul exemplified this as he expressed his gratefulness to the Philippians for the gift they sent him (Philippians 4:18). This type of brotherly gratitude can help us avoid offense and boost affection toward one another, especially when we are openly appreciative of the sacrifices other Christians make for us. It is especially effective when we show admiration when they least expect it.

Chapter 12

LUKEWARMNESS

To the angel of the church in Laodicea write: These are the words of
the Amen, the faithful and true witness, the ruler of God's creation.
I know your deeds, that you are neither cold nor hot. I wish you
were either one or the other! So, because you are lukewarm—
neither hot nor cold—I am about to spit you out of my mouth.

REVELATION 3:14–16, NIV

J ESUS SAYS IN Matthew 24:12–13 about the End Times, "Sin will be
rampant everywhere, and the love of many will grow cold. But the
one who endures to the end will be saved" (NLT). As ones who love
and follow Jesus, we need to watch out that our love does not run cold. If
it does, we will lose our salvation. Then everything we have been running
toward will be in vain.

We are warned again and again in the Bible against spiritual coldness or
lukewarmness. This is when God no longer occupies the number one spot
in our lives. Jesus cautions us against this in Luke 11:23; Elijah alerts us
of it in 1 Kings 18:21; James, in James 1:6–8; John, in John 12:42–43; and
Isaiah, in Isaiah 27:4–5, to name but a few. However, possibly the starkest
rebuke against this is in Revelation 3:15, quoted above. This is a shocking
statement, because Jesus is saying to some people in the church today that
He would prefer them to either be on fire for God, giving up everything

for Him and rendering 100 percent of themselves to Him, or be completely decided that they will not follow Him! It seems that Jesus does not accept half-hearted Christians. In fact, He says of them, "I will spew thee out of my mouth" (Rev. 3:16, KJV), showing how fed up He is with them and how we need to be on guard against this in our own lives.

Perhaps the reason Jesus cannot stand the lukewarm is because they are bad witnesses and hindrances for those saved, as well as for the unsaved. Just because we say we are doing something in God's name doesn't necessarily mean we are. Doing something in His name means we were directed by Him to do it, and in everything we do, we reflect Him. A rather extreme example is those who took part in the Inquisition in the thirteenth century. They called themselves Christians and believed they were doing God a service. Does this mean they really were by just believing in His existence but not turning to His ways? Jesus explains that some people murder, believing they are doing God's work (John 16:2).

It can be easy to be deceived by wealth and the belief that because one leads a prosperous, happy, and peaceful life, eternal destruction must be far away. This is exactly what happened to the church of Laodicea in Revelation 3:17. They were materially rich and lacking nothing, but spiritually they were paupers, without a penny to their name. Jesus urged them to wake up spiritually and completely change their ways (v. 18) and to repent (v. 19).

But perhaps the most common belief is that because someone seeks to do what is right and leads an "honest" life, he or she will go to heaven, regardless of having a relationship with God or not. However, as the Creator of the universe, God decides what is right and what is wrong. Just because someone thinks he is righteous does not necessarily mean he is when compared with God's high standard. He has decided to only allow those who believe in and obey Him to enter heaven, so living an upright life from our own point of view is not sufficient. Rather, we need to look at God's standards, ask forgiveness for falling short, and strive in obedience to His Word.

Lukewarmness is often a gradual and subtle process. We may start off our Christian lives on fire for God, seeking Him before everything with Him constantly on our mind. We have secured our place in heaven for the time being. Then, after a few months or years of churchgoing and Bible study, we gradually shut off to what is being preached at church. We lose our fire, or "first love," for God. We become complacent and indifferent to Him, although we would never admit it. Sometimes we would never even know to admit it because we may be unconscious of our true spiritual state.

This can often start as we desire more than our "spiritual bread." The Jews did this when they desired a different taste than the manna sent by God in the desert. They longed for the other foods from Egypt, something more than what God had given them. If we're no longer satisfied with what God is giving us, the problem is within us, not with God. Manna was enough to satisfy their hunger. The taste never changed, but they became fed up with the flavor. For us, Jesus says He is the manna from heaven. So when we start to dislike the taste of seeking Him, reading the Bible, praying, and spiritually feeding ourselves to be nearer our Lord, it means that we are starting to drift away from Him into spiritual apathy.

This reflects itself when we start desiring things other than the spiritual nutriment He has given us, such as thirsting for unspiritual distractions. When holiness no longer satisfies our soul as it did when we first grasped the depth and height of God's love, we may find we seek entertainment and diversion with the world, such as wanting to watch worldly films and television programs too much or developing an unhealthy desire for riches and material goods. We become aware that we have to have all the latest technology or the nicest house in the street, but not for a justified reason; we only want it to try and impress others or for self-satisfaction.

Often, this desire for riches turns into greed, and the desire for certain entertainment on the screen makes us desensitized to swearing, violence, nudity, sexual immorality, and gruesome and gory scenes. In fact, we may even find we become attracted to them. But Jesus warns us to be careful where we put our eyes (Luke 11:34, NLT), proving that these things can endanger our souls.

With regard to anything you watch on TV, if it's not useful for building you up in Christ, why watch it? Does it contain swearing? Does it contain the concept of fornication? If so, is it healthy to watch if it does not teach us a spiritual lesson? Followers of Christ should not observe many ungodly TV programs. We need to be on the lookout in our own attitudes for moral insensitivity, where we no longer listen to the Spirit of God and start to harden our hearts to the truth. Exposing ourselves to sin by viewing immoral contents on television or elsewhere is like someone under the old covenant presenting an animal sacrifice to God with defects and blemishes. Remember, "There is only one thing worth being concerned about" (Luke 10:42, NLT).

We may also find we waste hours and hours thinking about non-Christian affairs or issues, or perhaps amusing or entertaining ourselves in other non-spiritual activities when we could be seeking God and reading His Word. Our priorities radically but subtly change. God is no longer the first and foremost factor in our lives; our families may be, or our property, friends, free time, ministries, careers, or vacations—anything that distracts us from God's truth.

Another feature of our increased distance from God could be that our honesty sometimes slips. For example, we may find ourselves "borrowing" things from other people or institutions and never returning them or not being completely faithful to our word. Also, our pride and arrogance increases. We find ourselves ignoring some people. It is especially easy to ignore humble people. We no longer want to serve others but to be served. We demand respect from people and gossip about others behind their backs. We may harbor hardness in our hearts against certain people even for a very insignificant reason, although this is never justified because we are called to forgive just as Christ has forgiven us. We then find we have become more irritable and argumentative with people, including our friends and close family members, and even insensitive to their feelings.

We realize we complain about issues, including and especially other churches, our churches, leaders, people, and the government. We even gossip about people's possessions. Our day-to-day talk is no longer salty. We may notice ourselves chatting about unhelpful things with unwholesome dialogue and rude jokes. These offensive jokes that even many Christians may consider funny might not be blatantly rude in a sexual sense, but they can be filled with impurities, such as toilet humor or vileness that may make people feel sick but does not include swearing or outright immorality. Paul tells us we should have nothing to do with "filthiness, nor foolish talking, nor coarse jesting, which are not fitting, but rather giving of thanks. For this you know, that no fornicator, unclean person, nor covetous man, who is an idolater, has any inheritance in the kingdom of Christ and God" (Eph. 5:4–5).

Even more subtly than this, lukewarmness toward God can be reflected in what we eat. We stop caring about our bodies and begin to overeat, indulging the flesh in rich foods or too much of our favorite cuisine or snack. We also find we have not fasted for a very long time through spiritual disinterest. There is a huge but subtle difference between eating out of necessity and eating to indulge the flesh, including comfort eating; ingesting to escape from reality; and feeding ourselves to relieve stress, worry, or sadness. This is because when we do this, we are not trusting in or depending on God to fulfill us. We must be cautious about both eating in the extreme and also starving ourselves to the extreme (anorexia), because both feed the flesh.

These are but a few very well-hidden traits that often do not necessarily go directly against a specific biblical command but nonetheless reflect ungodliness. This makes them all the more deceitful and justified in the backslider's mind, and especially hard to detect. It is important to note that the traits described above can also belong to people who are regular churchgoers and may even be worship leaders or have a teaching or leadership role (1 Tim. 1:3, Titus 1:11).

Of course, the Christian described above may never outrightly deny Christ, and he or she may even evangelize regularly. He could be well respected in his Christian community because of all his good works and prayers in public. He may always pray before eating and could come from a Christian family. But to sum it up, he no longer walks in the Spirit but seeks to satisfy his fleshly and worldly desires. Because he may know all the Christian jargon and possibly watch Christian television, for example, nobody would ever class him as complacent, lukewarm, or a backslider, even though he has lost personal contact with God and his thought life and hidden personal life reflect this.

Jesus refers to the type of person described in Matthew 5:13 as someone who loses his or her saltiness: "You are the salt of the earth; but if the salt loses its flavor, how shall it be seasoned? It is then good for nothing but to be thrown out and trampled underfoot by men." This is quite a shocking statement. Complacency and lukewarmness toward God means we will "be thrown out and trampled by men"? That's really serious! Even in this state, we may easily carry on our daily Bible reading times, listen to Christian music, and visit the Christian bookstore. However, the fire and passion and hatred of sin are no longer there.

Jesus gives us an example of someone who decided not to be faithful with some responsibilities God gave him and consequently lost his salvation in Matthew 24:48–52.

> But what if the servant is evil and thinks, "My master won't be back for a while," and he begins beating the other servants, partying, and getting drunk? The master will return unannounced and unexpected, and he will cut the servant to pieces and assign him a place with the hypocrites. In that place there will be weeping and gnashing of teeth. (NLT)

So we must be careful not to commit ourselves halfheartedly but try our hardest to live holy lives in every area.

The story of David tells us how important it is to be constantly watching ourselves and our thoughts and actions, because sin could be dwelling in our hearts without realizing it. Then it will pounce on us and catch up to us, as it did with David when he sinned with Bathsheba. It is, in fact, easier to fall into sin and disobedience to God, than not to.

In order not to lose our salvation, we need to die every day to our own self-seeking conduct. Jesus says, "If any of you wants to be my follower, you must turn from your selfish ways, take up your cross, and follow me. If you try to hang on to your life, you will lose it. But if you give up your life for my sake and for the sake of the Good News, you will save it. And what do you benefit if you gain the whole world but lose your own soul?" (Mark 8:34–35, NLT). It is possible to turn from being the ruler of your own life and totally commit yourself to Jesus. Then, you will be saved. However, it is also possible to then, slowly and even without noticing it, take your life back and gradually start to live a selfish life, even though you may still be going to church every week and praying regularly, even working in the ministry full-time. If we allow this to happen, we will have lost our salvation. This is why we always need to examine our hearts and motives before God. If any selfishness and fleshly desires are there, we need to give them up to God and repent of them.

LOSING OUR SALVATION?

As a very young Christian, I always enjoyed reading the Bible, and by God's grace I still do. One day, a very admirable and Spirit-filled member of my congregation told me that it is impossible to lose your salvation. I stopped dead in my tracks. "Is that what the Bible says?" I wondered. I was sure I had read something different, but because I wasn't armed with any verses as a comeback, I lost the discussion. From then on I was always on the lookout for Bible verses either confirming the above statement or otherwise. Over time, I just could not believe how full the Bible is of verses warning exactly the opposite. It is easier to lose your salvation than to keep it. (Jesus warns us that hard work is needed; Luke 13:24.) One could fill a whole book on Bible verses proving this. But for the purposes of this book, I shall only display a few.

First of all, 2 Peter 2:20–22 says:

> For if, after they have escaped the pollutions of the world through the knowledge of the Lord and Savior Jesus Christ, they are again entangled in them and overcome, the latter end is worse for them than the beginning. For it would have been better for them not to have known the way of righteousness, than having known it, to turn from the holy commandment delivered to them. But it has happened to them according to the true proverb: "A dog returns

to his own vomit," and, "a sow, having washed, to her wallowing in the mire."

Some people insist that the people Peter is talking about above never really experienced genuine salvation; they thought it was, but their lack of perseverance proves they did not know God personally. (See the parable of the sower; Matt. 13:18–23). However, there is no evidence to support this interpretation. Peter does not write that they *believed* they knew Christ. He wrote that they had actually escaped the corruption of the world. Notice the word *again* comes before *entangled in them*; if they went back to their sinful life again, then they must have genuinely left it in the first place. Peter did not write that these people merely presumed they knew the Savior. They did actually know Him, according to verse 20, but they then turned their backs on Him. Peter goes on to say that it would have been better if they had not known the way in the first place. This is because it is referring to the punishment that is coming to such people who turn away from the truth. Jesus warns, " If anyone does not abide in Me, he is cast out as a branch and is withered; and they gather them and throw them into the fire, and they are burned" (John 15:6).

To support this theory, let's see what else Jesus says. He starts by telling us that it is not easy to enter heaven.

> Work hard to enter the narrow door to God's Kingdom, for many will try to enter but will fail. When the master of the house has locked the door, it will be too late. You will stand outside knocking and pleading, "Lord, open the door for us!" But he will reply, "I don't know you or where you come from." Then you will say, "But we ate and drank with you, and you taught in our streets." And he will reply, "I tell you, I don't know you or where you come from. Get away from me, all you who do evil."
> —LUKE 13:24–27, NLT

From this we learn that some of those who think they are going to heaven, those who call God "Lord," who hear the Word of God preached regularly, and who take Communion, will actually not enter. Jesus shows us that doing evil is enough to disqualify ourselves from His kingdom. Again this is supported in Romans 2:7–9, where Paul wrote:

> He will give eternal life to those who keep on doing good, seeking after the glory and honor and immortality that God offers. But he will pour out his anger and wrath on those who live for them-selves, who refuse to obey the truth and instead live lives of wickedness. There will be trouble and calamity for everyone who keeps on doing what is evil. (NLT)

So if someone becomes a Christian, then decides not to obey the truth and dies without repentance, he or she will be subject to God's wrath.

People use John 10:28 against the belief that salvation is losable. It says, "I give them eternal life, and they shall never perish; neither shall anyone snatch them out of My hand." I deem that this verse refers to everyone who has already died in Christ, that is, all people who have already passed from this world into the next. It does not refer to you and me, people who have not yet died. Jesus is saying that those who have passed the test by dying faithful to Him and have entered into eternal life shall not perish in the flames of hell and will never be taken away from Him.

Romans 8:29–30 is also used in supporting the idea that salvation is not losable: "For whom He foreknew, He also predestined to be conformed to the image of His Son, that He might be the firstborn among many brethren. Moreover whom He predestined, these He also called; whom He called, these He also justified; and whom He justified, these He also glorified." Where predestination and hence the grace of God are dominant themes in the Old and New Testaments (Gen. 25:23; Acts 13:48), the Bible still shows us that we have free will. We make our own choices and decisions. Our attitudes and actions that we have complete control over in our own lives decide whether we have been predestined as children of God or not. Whoever obeys Jesus on Earth was naturally chosen in Christ before the creation of the world (Eph. 1:4). We also read in the Bible that names can be erased from the Book of Life (Ps. 69:28; Matt. 25:29).

Even Paul was fearful about losing his salvation and worked as hard as he could so as not to lose it, writing, "I discipline my body like an athlete, training it to do what it should. Otherwise, I fear that after preaching to others I myself might be disqualified" (1 Cor. 9:27, NLT). He also warns his precious church in Rome about it: "Notice how God is both kind and severe. He is severe toward those who disobeyed, but kind to you if you continue to trust in his kindness. But if you stop trusting, you also will be cut off" (Rom. 11:22, NLT).

In order not to become seduced by lukewarmness and therefore lose our salvation, the rest of this chapter deals with biblical ways to overcome it.

WATCHFULNESS

One way is to keep spiritually alert and watchful in prayer. A key element of the Christian life is to be on the lookout and guard our hearts and minds against temptations and the schemes of the devil. We need to mind our thought lives at all times. We may often find our minds wandering toward worldly lusts, so we constantly need to be spiritually awake to steer ourselves away. This can happen anywhere—at church, in the streets, in the supermarket, relaxing with friends, or at home. We all know what our weaknesses are, whether it be a certain person who influences us negatively, a certain shop which makes us desire material things, a certain web site, a certain restaurant that makes us greedy, certain music (even Christian music) we find ourselves idolizing, a certain time during the evening when a particular type of TV program is being aired that makes us lustful or greedy for worldly things. We need to be vigilant at all times against these things. We must always be checking our motives and desires and constantly be aware of our thought lives and actions. One day God could be the most important aspect of our lives and the following day situations or circumstances can change or opportunities can arise, and God suddenly no longer has the number one spot. Remember that Satan wants more than anything to rob us of our salvation.

Jesus actually describes praying as watching. In the Garden of Gethsemane, during prayer time, some of the disciples fell asleep. He challenged them, "Couldn't you watch with me even one hour? Keep watch and pray, so that you will not give in to temptation" (Matt. 26:40–41, NLT). Jesus knows of man's temptation to be disloyal during times of difficulty, especially before a violent situation such as the one He was about to endure, or when our comfort zone is squeezed; so, He counsels us to be spiritually awake, watching out for evil temptations and not succumbing to the desires of the flesh, which in the passage above is represented by the disciples' sleeping.

He commands us to pray, asking God for protection from temptation and for strength not to be overcome by evil. Jesus repeats this in Revelation 3:2–3, in a different situation, in the face of a spiritually dead church: "Be watchful, and strengthen the things which remain, that are ready to die: for I have not found thy works perfect before God. Remember therefore how thou hast received and heard, and hold fast, and repent. If therefore thou shalt not watch, I will come on thee as a thief, and thou shalt not know what hour I will come upon thee" (KJV). Whatever situation we are faced with, whether it be a time of plenty or a time or lack, whether it be a difficult time in our lives or one of ease, Jesus warns us to remain vigilant against the schemes of the devil and to never stop praying. As mentioned above, we need to always keep our thoughts, words, and actions in check at all times. (See the section entitled "Resisting Temptation" in Chapter 6.)

ETERNAL PERSPECTIVE

When Jesus was challenged about whether it was right to pay taxes or not, He replied, "Give to Caesar what belongs to Caesar, and give to God what belongs to God" (Mark 12:17, NLT). This answer absolutely amazed His listeners and shamed His accusers. Through such a reply, Jesus challenges us to view the world through God's eyes, not from a human viewpoint. The Pharisees who posed Him this question were green with jealousy and were seeking to please man and report Jesus to the authorities. If Jesus had agreed to pay taxes, the Pharisees would have accused Him of being a traitor of the Jewish nation. If He had disagreed, they would have denounced Him to the Herodians and ordered Him to be arrested. Jesus saw through their hypocrisy and used the opportunity to teach you and me that everything we do, every opportunity that presents itself to us, should be used to glorify God.

In addition to this, Jesus invites us to view life from the spiritual side of things. When we pay our taxes, we shouldn't do it resentfully because we will have less money afterwards. We ought to just get on with paying them and dedicate our lives to glorifying God. Jesus is saying that worldly rules and regulations are not important, although we must obey them when they don't contradict God's laws. What matters is what is unseen, our hearts, our motives, and our actions before the Lord. Rather than viewing the world in the physical realm, we must see it from an eternal perspective and live for God in everything we do. (See Chapter 10, "Riches.")

Jesus also always focused His gaze on the future reward, not on the problem at hand. When the Jewish elders questioned Jesus as to His identity during His trial, His answer was, "If I tell you, you will not believe me, and if I asked you, you would not answer. But from now on, the Son of Man will be seated at the right hand of the mighty God" (Luke 22:67–69, NIV). The Lord knew what a glorious future was awaiting Him and that in order to get there He still had a horrific death to go through. So as to strengthen Himself and quicken His destiny, He looked upon the situation through heaven's eyes.

We are also told in the Bible, in Revelation 20:12, that everything we do is recorded, and we will be judged according to it: "I saw the dead, both great and small, standing before God's throne. And the books were opened, including the Book of Life. And the dead were judged according to what they had done, as recorded in the books" (NLT). If we keep this in mind everyday, we find we will act very differently, and our attitudes will change. Paul exhorted such living by advising the Philippians to keep their eyes on their heavenward goal, which is receiving eternal crowns and spending eternity with Christ.

> I press on toward the goal to win the prize for which God has called me heavenward in Christ Jesus.
> —PHILIPPIANS 3:14, NIV

SOAKING OURSELVES IN GOD'S TRUTH AND LOVE

Sing and make music in your heart to the Lord, always giving thanks to God the Father for everything, in the name of our Lord Jesus Christ.

—EPHESIANS 5:19–20, NIV

We need to make sure we are not spiritual parasites, as the Israelites were, where all our prayers consist of is asking for things. Out of sheer love for Him and satisfaction in Him, we should praise the Lord voluntarily, bask in His presence, drink His living water, and worship Him with all our hearts, singing spiritual songs and enjoying who He is. It is an excellent idea and very wise to have a specific time or times in the day set apart exclusively to spend time with God. Getting into a habit like this does wonders for spiritual growth. Daniel did this three times a day (Dan. 6:10).

Israel never admired God for who He was but more for what He did. They were hardly ever grateful and rarely praised Him of their own accord. We must be careful not to fall into this mistake of dissatisfaction with God. The whole chapter of 1 Corinthians 10 tells us where the Hebrews erred and that they were spiritually cold toward the Lord Almighty. When we, too, start to feel unsatisfied and wish things were different—for example, that the church service were longer or shorter or that different songs were sung—we must go back to our roots and just be fulfilled in Him.

Chapter 13

SPIRITUAL MATURITY

*And this is my prayer: that your love may abound more and
more in knowledge and depth of insight, so that you may be able
to discern what is best and may be pure and blameless until the
day of Christ, filled with the fruit of righteousness that comes
through Jesus Christ—to the glory and praise of God.*

PHILIPPIANS 1:9–11

S PIRITUAL MATURITY IS knowing God (1 John 2:13), which is achieved
by living in complete purity and total obedience to Him. This
involves death to the flesh and having such an intimate relationship
with Him that our favorite and regular activity is adoring Him. Its definition is basically knowing how to act to please God in every minute detail of
one's life and also having the ability and grace to do it. Instead of committing frequent sins, we walk in righteousness all the time before absolutely
everyone, full of humility and wisdom. The Christian life is one in which
growth is or should be more or less constant. Whoever we are, there will
always be more room for progress, and if someone thinks even for a second
they are spiritually mature, it is nearly always the start of their downfall
and probably means they are most likely committing the sin of pride.

Christians grow into spiritual maturity as they increase in godly wisdom
and knowledge of His will. Such maturity is characterized by an abundance

of love toward God and all men. True *agape* love, overflowing and always increasing, is the essence of Christian adulthood. As we get closer to God and we learn more about Him from an intimate relationship and also through study of His Word, the natural effect is the development of the fruit of love. This is not airy-fairy love but profound love that is reached through insight and understanding. As God works this process in us, we will be able to determine the way we are to live as pure and faultless people before a perfect God. Therefore, one of the Christian's ultimate goals will be achieved—God will be glorified through our righteousness and good sense as we shine out as beacons of light in this dark world.

This mature love manifests itself in different ways toward other believers. One outcome of it is unity in the body of Christ (Eph. 4:16). As Jesus has distributed different spiritual gifts to His people, they come together in the unity of love and are able to work in harmony to do God's will, overlooking each other's faults (Eph. 4:2). The apostle Paul demonstrates this using the anatomy of the human body in 1 Corinthians 12. Any part of the human body on its own cannot survive, just as any section of Christ's body is unable to individually carry out God's work. It is almost as good as useless. It needs the support and diversity of the other members (Eph. 4:11–12) to carry out good purposes. This unification of such differing members witnesses to the world that God's love is in us (John 17:23). Mature love also creates a deep respect for each member and a fear of God to take orders from Him as the head.

Another fruit of spiritual development and oneness is the ability to speak the truth to one another in love (Eph. 4:15). This concept is clearly explained in Galatians 6:1: "Brothers, if someone is caught in a sin, you who are spiritual should restore him gently" (NIV). Notice the Word of God tells us to be gentle. If this is not done in a kind manner, the brother may be offended or feel humiliated, and it could cause them to rebel even more. We must always be wise about the way in which we address sensitive subjects; otherwise, it could break the unison. And we need to make sure we have a Bible verse on the ready to softly prove what they are doing is contrary to right living.

When Jesus had dinner in the home of a leader of the Pharisees in Luke

14:7–3, His correction was channeled toward those who claim to follow God, but through spiritual pride and shortsightedness, do not. In Jesus' day, this was the Pharisees, and today it is some of us in the church. Instead of teaching them about mercy and love, Jesus corrects their erroneous beliefs and practices, revealing their hypocrisy and showing them the way of humility so they might change their attitudes.

Both love and wisdom are gifts from God that develop as we grow in the Christian faith. Wisdom, essential for living a life of holiness, begins with the fear of the Lord (Isa. 33:6) and leads to a better knowledge of God (Eph. 1:17) and knowing and executing His will (Col. 1:9). It is also a superior understanding of spiritual things, not only factual but practical, equipping us to give advice and share insight regarding everyday life in the faith. The wisdom in Proverbs and the wisdom Jesus teaches, for example, both give down-to-Earth advice for everyday situations and teach the student discipline with understanding.

> Anyone who listens to my teaching and follows it is wise, like a person who builds a house on solid rock.
> —MATTHEW 7:24, NLT

Wisdom is also about being perfected in Christ, so that everything we do is for him. James wrote, "But the wisdom that comes from heaven is first of all pure; then peace-loving, considerate, submissive, full of mercy and good fruit, impartial and sincere" (James 3:17, NIV). It is also knowing how to instruct others about the right ways and speaking out God's truth. God-given wisdom also leads to living a fruitful life that honors and glorifies God in all areas and circumstances (Col. 1:10). Wisdom and love equip us to endure times of trials, temptations, and difficulties with patience.

Wisdom also takes us along the path of having our hope firmly rooted in the gospel, as God reveals to us His glorious power and great might (Eph. 1:18). God gives this gift to those who have the Spirit of God in them (1 Cor. 2:11–15), the humble (James 3:13), and the obedient (Eccles. 8:5).

Let's take a look at the parable of the ten bridesmaids. Half of the bridesmaids took enough oil for the lamps, and the other half were foolish and did not. The five foolish ones missed the arrival of the bridegroom because they did not have enough oil. They then were not allowed to enter the wedding feast. The bridegroom shouted to them, "Assuredly, I say to you, I do not know you" (Matt. 25:12).

This is a metaphor about all people who call themselves Christians. Some are wise, keep watch, and have enough oil in their lamps. In other words, they feed on God's Word daily and live a holy, Spirit-filled life according to the Bible. This group is represented as the five wise bridesmaids. There are many people in the church who do not seek God. They live "normal" lives, just as the world does, except they call themselves Christians and outwardly do what Christians do. They attend church and are waiting for Jesus' return. Without realizing it, mostly because they are living to please themselves and not God, they are not saved, although they think they are. They may pray out loud in church, say they love God, and have the gift of miracles; however, without living a holy life and therefore keeping oil in their lamps, they are not saved. Does it shock you to know that 50 percent of the people in your church may not be saved? We need to ask ourselves if we are one of them.

The writer of Hebrews has much to say about believers who keep on drinking spiritual milk, which serves for spiritual sloths who do not progress in their faith, rather than digesting proper spiritual food (Heb. 5:12–13). The spiritually immature are those who do not have the knowledge to distinguish between right and wrong, he says. He tries to encourage them to stop going over and over the basics of the Christian faith and to advance to the meatier parts—love, knowledge, wisdom, patience, and righteousness. However, this can only be done with God's help, not by human effort alone (Heb. 6:3). This stresses the importance of praying for spiritual growth, studying the Bible, and calling out to God for Him to give us wisdom. However, we must learn from the story of Solomon that while it is prudent to ask for wisdom, wisdom alone does not save. We should also ask for grace to follow through what our God-given wisdom tells us.

ENDURANCE IN SUFFERING

We must through many tribulations enter the kingdom of God.

—ACTS 14:22

The Scriptures warn us that if we choose to follow Christ, suffering will certainly await us (2 Tim. 3:12; Rom. 8:17–18) in one form or another. While persecution is not easy and can lead to difficulties and sorrow, God's Word teaches us there are some advantages to it.

Suffering has a refining effect. Romans 5:3–4 shows us that persecution helps develop character, endurance, and trust in God. James says suffering from religious discrimination cultivates perseverance, leading to spiritual maturity (James 1:2–4). Through our troubles, we will experience Christ's comfort (2 Cor. 1:4–6), to the praise, glory, and honor of Jesus (1 Pet. 1:7). God Almighty also allows suffering in order to draw us closer to Him because hurt can turn our thoughts to Him, for both Christians and non-Christians. He is our Rock and proves Himself a tower of strength when adversity arises (Ps. 18:2).

Jesus instructs us to, in fact, celebrate during hardships because of our eternal reward awaiting us (Luke 6:23). The apostles, after having been whipped for the first time because of their evangelism, were "rejoicing that they were counted worthy to suffer shame for His name" (Acts 5:41). We are therefore supposed to regard trials and persecutions as valuable, for through them God will be glorified and honored, although it is not always an easy process to arrive at this state of mind. We must view hard times as a chance to prove to God we're firm in Him as we stand in His patience with our eyes focused on Him.

We ought to even be ready to unjustly suffer for doing good and acting righteously in a fallen world. Many people are offended and confused at the Christian life of selflessness and living for God, and because of this we will be ridiculed and attacked for being different. If we take offense at this, even from family members and close friends, we are acting unjustifiably. We must remember to keep quiet, trust in God, and have a joyful attitude in the midst of our agony. When it is very necessary to answer or talk with the people mistreating us, we should always demonstrate humility and stick to the Word of God.

We should also prepare our minds as best as possible for the possibility of suffering, not just mental abuse in the form of words, but physical abuse, too. Paul suffered hunger, thirst, a lack of sleep, beatings, imprisonments, poverty, and sorrow (2 Cor. 6:5, 10). Jesus advises us that those who suffer poverty, hunger, sadness, hatred, and mockery because of the good news are blessed and await a wonderful reward (Luke 6:20–22). We should even expect some of these things in order to enter the kingdom of heaven and should prayerfully ask God to protect us against falling away as soon as difficulties arise.

When we do suffer physically, it distances us from sin because life's priorities radically shift when our well-being is in danger. The changed attitude that suffering in the flesh brings about actually draws us closer to God as the reality of how delicate and short our time on Earth is rings home. Suffering can therefore make us more ready to press on toward the goal of carrying out God's will (1 Pet. 4:2).

Paul, a bit of a genius at handling suffering, reflected on Christ's infinite and unfailing love, which supports and strengthens us in the face of troubles (Rom. 8:35–36). God equips us with the ability to endure suffering and will not allow us to undergo more than we can bear. Those who fall away because of suffering, whether unfair or not, do not have their love deeply rooted in Christ's and certainly have not reached spiritual maturity.

In order to persevere under hardships, Paul calls on an eternal perspective—looking at the grand scheme of things in comparison with one's own problems and pains and focusing on the spiritual side of the battles being won as we patiently endure suffering (2 Cor. 4:17–18). According to the physical side, we will experience grief and afflictions, but we must view these as transitory and focus on our actions and attitudes in the spiritual realm.

Compared to our everlasting reward and eternal glory, Paul sees his troubles as insignificant (Rom. 8:18). To name but a few of these rewards, we will receive the crown of life (Rev. 2:10), the authority to rule over the nations (Rev. 2:26–27), our names written in the Book of Life, acknowledgement by

Jesus before the Father (Rev. 3:5), the right to sit with Jesus on His throne (Rev. 3:21), Jesus' new name written on us (Rev. 3:12), and free drink from the spring of the water of life as our inheritance (Rev. 21:6–7).

Even today, many, many people are severely persecuted, even to death, for being Christians. This is happening now in North Korea and in communist China, where believers are tortured and countless house churches are shut down. In order to give us hope in times of suffering, Peter points out that our present agony is a temporary state, while our reward in heaven—where there is no affliction—is eternal (1 Pet. 1:4, 6).

Paul refined the art of fortitude under persecution. His solution is very simple: contentment always, whatever the situation. He could maintain this attitude because he knew his strength came from Jesus, in order for him to carry out God's will (Philippians 4:12–13). The source of this strength is God's dedicated love and grace. Paul knew that alone he could do nothing and relied on God for absolutely everything. That is why he rested in the truth that God's power is perfected in weakness (2 Cor. 12:9). This was an amazing discovery, considering he had withstood almost every sort of adversity through this method—trouble from natural disasters, from other people's sinfulness, from governmental corruption, backstabbing from brothers, divisions within some of the churches, among many others. When we really understand that because of our weaknesses we can do everything God wants us to do through His power in us, He will give us the stamina and courage to overcome any form of mistreatment.

James reminds his readers in James 5:10–11 of the prophets' and Job's model examples of enduring under hardship and of Job's final reward, which left him far richer than before his suffering. No one can deny that Job complained and lamented his dreadful situation, but just before the end of his ordeal, although God reprimands Job for speaking about what he did not understand, God calls Job His servant and declares that Job spoke correctly about Him. Amidst nightmarish and seemingly unjust circumstances, Job does not blaspheme or lose his faith but continues to steadfastly trust the Lord with impatient and desperate perseverance. Despite Job's bitterness, discouragement, and depression, he won the battle of faith. In his own words, "Yet the righteous will hold to his way, And he who has clean hands will be stronger and stronger" (Job 17:9).

PERSEVERANCE

> You need to persevere so that when you have done the will of God, you will receive what he has promised. For in just a very little while, "He who is coming will come and will not delay."
> —HEBREWS 10:36–37, NIV

Perseverance is one of those characteristics that if we lack it will cause us to lose our way on the pathway to life and therefore not be permitted access to enter heaven (Matt. 10:22). Jesus warns that in the End Times, which is now, many will desert the faith and turn to hatred. Wickedness will increase, and love will decrease (Matt. 24:10–12). All this going on around us will boost the temptation to give up our first love and become lukewarm. Persecution is also an inducement to not hold on, but we must hang on to the truth to be saved. Lack of determination was a reality for the disciples, too. Jesus prayed for Simon Peter's faith not to miscarry in Luke 22:32.

King Asa was one of the five more godly kings of Judah in the Books of Kings and Chronicles. He started off his reign as a blessing to the people. He cleansed the land of idolatry and ordered them to seek God. He also experienced God's hand with him in battle as he called and relied on the Lord for victory against Zerah the Cushite (2 Chron. 14:11). Asa was obviously a man after God's own heart. However, he lacked one thing—perseverance.

Unfortunately, Asa's steadfastness and zeal failed. Instead of trusting in God at the threat of war as he had done before, he confided in the help of another king and used riches from the Lord's temple to bribe him. Asa never again turned to God, not even at death's door. Plus, he sinned by ruthlessly oppressing some of the people (2 Chron. 16:10). The first half of his reign and his relationship with God were tremendous. The second part of his rule was a complete failure because his determination and strength of purpose faltered. He lost sight of God and seemed to forget Him, going from one extreme to the other.

How did such a godly man backslide? Why did he not persist in his faith? More than likely, he did not keep watch. The Word of God tells us to be on guard against evil, which wants to take our salvation away from us (Acts 20:31). We need to pray we do not fall into temptation (Luke 22:46) and always make sure we are desiring the right things, like prayer, Bible study, church, and fellowship with the saints, not worldly distractions that feed the flesh. God's Word also tells us to pray without ceasing (1 Thess. 5:17) and that His Word feeds the soul (Matt. 4:4). Do you eat food every day? Yes, because you need it. We should also be digesting spiritual food daily, because our souls crave it. Maybe Asa lost the habit of praying, and perhaps he got lazy and stopped seeking God. He must have lost his dedication to reading and hearing God's truth and Word. Maybe he found his comfort zone and got comfortable; he let the pleasures of this world take over because he wasn't prepared with the armor of God for the day of battle. Then, when the day of testing arrived, he decided to trust in a man instead of relying on the living God.

In Jesus' words, persevering is remaining in Him. We need to remain in the Vine with Him as our head, which is living in obedience to His Word. Asa stopped remaining in Him and ceased to eat the manna that came down from heaven. He gave up on taking Jesus' living water (John 4:12–13) and bread from heaven (John 6:35). In order to nourish ourselves on these good things, we must partake in regular Bible study time, prayer, and fellowship with the church. This is how we overcome (1 John 2:14).

Another major contributing factor to Asa's spiritual downfall was probably that he forgot all God had done in his life. He failed to remember his experiences with God, what the taste of God's love was like, the Lord's goodness, and His presence. Forgetfulness is an enemy of perseverance, as it erases our knowledge of Immanuel. We are left with no reason or motivation to pursue the faith. Throughout the Old Testament, there is a lot of repetition of Israel's history and God's laws. In the beginning of Deuteronomy, Moses runs a huge recap of everything that happened with him as leader. This underlines the importance of never forgetting what God has done in our lives so as not to return to the same erroneous ways. Moses also gives the Jews a warning, "Only be careful, and watch yourselves closely so that you do not forget the things your eyes have seen or let them slip from your heart as long as you live. Teach them to your children and to their children after them. Remember the day you stood before the LORD your God" (Deut. 4:9–10, NIV). Moses was aware that by burying what God had done, Israel would very quickly break faith.

From beginning to end in Israel's history, the Hebrews evidently coped much better in times of difficulty than during the prosperous years. During the successful, easy times, they gave themselves over to materialism and riches instead of to God (Amos 3:15). When the going got tough and their comfort zones were squeezed, then they would remember the Lord their God and seek Him, and so were rescued from their troubles. We need to be careful not to do the same. It can be easy to lose perseverance and forget God when things are going well for us because we feel like we do not need Him and can cope on our own. But when we remember the captivity and spiritual darkness from whence we came and how much freer we are now, we should be able to hold on to His truth more firmly. However, there is a danger of clutching on to the past too much, recalling it too often, and bringing up unhelpful memories. Christians only need to look at the past to remember the wonderful things God has done for them, not for any other purpose, because Jesus has forgiven our sins and wiped our slate clean.

Proof of perseverance in the life of the Christian is bearing fruit, the result of working hard at our salvation. Redemption is a gift from God that we receive when we decide to follow and obey Jesus, and it involves a sanctifying process. Paul describes it as a race in which we work and train hard like athletes to reach the prize (1 Cor. 9:24–27). Another outcome of persevering is the works that come from faith. The Scriptures tell us that we reap what we sow, meaning that when we do evil, we will end up in hell; and when we do good according to the Spirit of God, we will go to heaven (Gal. 6:7–9). We must make every effort to please and be charitable toward everyone, especially the family of believers (v. 10), as we strive to remain in Christ.

Peter encourages perseverance in the faith in order for his readers to affirm they have been chosen by God to receive salvation from Jesus Christ. This will help them not to fall and to stay firm (2 Pet. 1:10–12). This persistence is characterized by growth in the faith, perfecting the qualities of goodness, knowledge, self-control, perseverance, godliness, kindness, and love (2 Pet. 1:5–7).

Love is the secret to success in the Christian race. Remaining strong in our relationship with God comes about by doing "everything in love" (1 Cor. 16:14). When we hold firmly to our first love and keep Him in sight constantly, it will be hard not to persevere. This will help us to never tire of doing good (2 Thess. 3:13). Love also brings about unity in the church, strengthening each member.

We must remember to never be afraid of our enemies, but to keep the fear of the Lord close to our hearts as we believe that He has the power to kill the body and then throw our soul into hellfire. Make resisting the devil an art (James 4:7), always being dressed in the armor of God, and give reason for the enemy to fear you. Always trust in God and in His faithfulness to strengthen and protect you from the devil (2 Thess. 3:3).

David soldiered on, despite trouble on all sides. When his enemies were all he could see before him and all he could hear was their scorn, he still planted his hope in and fixed his thoughts on the Lord (Ps. 69:12–20). He knew that his only chance of survival was in God, so he matured in his faith and relationship with God, enduring to the end.

While there is a large human element to firmness in the faith, we must not forget that we also rely on God and the part He has to play in our sanctification. Without His gracious hand stretched out over us, there is no growth, no matter how hard we try. The grace of God in our lives is what enables and empowers us to execute His will and be steadfast (1 Cor. 15:10). He is the one who begins, continues, and completes our salvation, never us by ourselves (Philippians 1:6). God's grace builds us up and takes us through to eternal life, and this only happens with those who strive in their Christian life.

FASTING

> But the days will come when the bridegroom will be taken away
> from them, and then they will fast.
>
> —MATTHEW 9:15

Through reading the Bible and especially the New Testament, no one can deny that fasting must be part of a Christian's life. In Matthew 6:16, Jesus starts talking about fasting by saying, "Moreover, when you fast..." Rather than "if you fast" or "if you want to fast," He uses *when*, revealing that fasting is a part of following Christ, not an optional extra. In this passage, Jesus instructs us to hide the fact that we are fasting from others, rather than announce it.

> But when you fast, comb your hair and wash your face. Then
> no one will notice that you are fasting, except your Father, who
> knows what you do in private. And your Father, who sees every-
> thing, will reward you.
>
> —MATTHEW 6:17–18, NLT

In the Old Testament times, fasting was used to implore divine power to escape disaster, such as the decree for the death of all Jews in the Book of Esther, and it also represented self-denial, humility, repentance, and mourning. This was often abused by the Israelites, who accompanied fasting with an impure heart, wickedness, and a lack of humility (Isa. 58:3–4). Even for us, abstinence from food can be used as a religious show, and it is unacceptable before God when it is accompanied with a self-seeking, carnal lifestyle without humility. God condemns those who fast in order to show their humbleness, yet explains that when they do not fast, they are as proud as the wicked (Isa. 58). Fasting should be accompanied by a life of holiness, not just a day. Before we fast, we need a time of self-reflection and examination to ensure we are leading a life of purity before a holy God. Jesus communicated that fasting is only to be executed when we are "new skins" (Luke 5:34–39), meaning that abstinence from food is of spiritual benefit only to those born again by the Holy Spirit.

Jesus used fasting as a tool in spiritual battle to overcome temptation and subdue sin (Matt. 4). It gave Him power and authority in the spiritual world as He vanquished the flesh and subjected Himself completely to God's will. We can use fasting in the same way as we battle against sin's power and overcome impurity in our lives. It is also powerful to break the dominion of darkness reigning in people, nations, and governments, and it sets people free from their bondage to sin, bringing them into the light; therefore, we should use it when praying for salvation. In Mark 9:29, Jesus reveals that fasting along with prayer and faith can set people free from the clasp of the powers of darkness as it gives us authority to expel demons from people's lives.

In the New Testament, fasting is also used at times of spiritual significance, such as by Paul at the time of his conversion and at the time of appointing elders and missionaries in the early church in Acts. The Bible does not specify what type of food or drink was abstained from or the length of the fast, but we need to make sure our fast consists of real sacrifices on our part, rather than abstaining from certain foods we would not be eating or do not like anyway.

SERVANT HEART

> Whoever wants to be a leader among you must be your servant, and whoever wants to be first among you must become your slave.
>
> —MATTHEW 20:26–27, NLT

Servants in Jesus' day were the most humble members of a household, looked down upon by the majority and given the most menial jobs. They did nothing of their own accord or will; all they did was receive orders and carry them out all day long without complaining or hesitation. When corrected or reprimanded, they did not answer back and were extra careful never to commit the same error again. In everything they selflessly gave their all to please their master.

At the Last Supper, as told in John 13, Jesus put a towel around His waist, giving Him the appearance of a slave, and proceeded to wash His disciples' feet, an act that only servants carried out, certainly never the guest of honor. This job required the slave to kneel on the floor and bend over, touching with care the lowest, dirtiest, and probably the most unattractive part of the body. To do this twelve consecutive times in one sitting takes patience and dedication. After each washing, the water would have been dirty, so Jesus would have had to change it twelve times—very time-consuming. Jesus took this humbling task upon Himself as an example of the kind of role Christians should play for one another, serving one another and taking on servile and submissive tasks for each other's comfort.

In any society, over all time, it would be absurd that the most honored guest, and a King, would take on the role of a slave. This is why only the spiritually mature are able to take on such humble roles. The equivalent nowadays may be discreetly picking up garbage after a church meeting; helping clear up after visitors in someone's home; having people who can't pay us back around for dinner (Luke 14:12–13); and volunteering our services for unglamorous jobs, such as helping someone to do their gardening, painting their house, taking on general household chores, or coaching for free—basically giving our time to other believers in service, with no reward.

A very short time after washing the disciples' feet, Jesus went on to do something even more mind-blowing. The perfect Creator of the universe laid down His life in love for undeserving mankind on the cross at Calvary. This supreme act of sacrificial, selfless love serves as a perfect example of taking on the worst mission imaginable for the benefit of other people. Jesus served all who are saved with His body and blood, the accomplishment of a truly humble and faithful servant to humanity. And yet He is King! Jesus put aside His glory and "made himself nothing, taking the very nature of a servant" (Philippians 2:7, NIV). As our perfect example to follow (Eph. 5:1), we too must have this same nature of self-sacrificial love and lowliness.

This is the complete opposite of what the world teaches. The world sometimes thinks that whoever is in charge can lord it over those underneath them. Jesus turns this on its head and says that whoever is great, must be a servant (Mark 10:42–45). The core of the Christian character is humility. We must never think of ourselves or act more importantly than our brother, especially if we have a more distinguished role. Before God, we are all of equal value (Rom. 2:11). In fact, whoever does have a particular role within the church should try the hardest to find deeds of servanthood to carry out. In that way, on the day of Christ's return, they will be exalted rather than humbled (Matt. 23:11–12), as Christ is now exalted at the Father's right hand.

VIGILANCE FOR JESUS' RETURN

You also must be ready all the time, for the Son of Man will come when least expected.

—MATTHEW 24:44, NLT

Anticipating Jesus' second coming should radically affect our behavior and stance on life. When we really believe that He could return any minute, we will be convicted that anything we do that does not honor Him or put Him above everything else is unavailing. As we eagerly await Christ's return, we must likewise be aware of our upcoming judgment, a serious motivation for holy and godly living in the fear of the Lord. Peter's advice is to have clear-mindedness and self-control in order to lead a life of prayer (1 Pet. 4:7). Christians should also consequently be faithful with their spiritual gifts for the benefit of others and the glory of God (1 Pet. 4:9–11). James urges them to be "patient and stand firm" in James 5:8 (NIV).

The exhortation to be prepared in Matthew 24:44 refers to watching our every move to make sure we do not offend the Holy Spirit. This includes always making sure we have forgiven other people, leaving no debt of forgiveness outstanding, and also asking for forgiveness in instances of offense. To sum up, we must try our hardest at living in peace with everyone. The secret of this is loving one another with Christ's love because love leads to forgiveness and humility. This attentiveness for His return urges us to take up all opportunities to do good and share our faith, knowing what will happen to those who do not follow Jesus.

One sign of backsliding is when the thought of Jesus' second coming doesn't excite us and when we believe it won't be for a long time (Matt. 24:48; 1 Thess. 5:3). Those who are found to be unwatchful on that day will not enter the kingdom of God (Matt. 25:1–13).

The Bible is very clear in indicating the impossibility of predicting the exact hour of the King's return. Some, in their enthusiasm, try to foretell when this will be, but any predictions will be wrong, as Jesus tells us He will come back when least expected. Paul underscores Jesus' teaching, saying, "For you yourselves know perfectly that the day of the Lord so comes as a thief in the night" (1 Thess. 5:2). The fact that someone has guessed a certain date means that will certainly not be it!

However, certain signs have been indicated, such as the increase in travel and knowledge (Dan. 12:4). With the extremely rapid increase in technology from the last century until now, including space travel and the development of computers and mobile phones, and with more and more people taking trips in airplanes, high-speed boats, high-speed trains, cars, and buses, no one can deny that we are living in the Last Days. Another sign Jesus indicates is the increase in wars, earthquakes, and famine (Matt. 24:6–8). One only needs to watch the news to see these are on the increase right now. With the second coming so imminent in our generation, it gives us all the more reason to be on guard and stand firm in the faith (1 Cor. 16:13–14).

Jesus' return marks the day we will receive our salvation (Heb. 9:28), when we will be judged and rewarded according to our works (1 Cor. 3:12–15), and when we will receive the crown of righteousness (2 Tim. 4:8) and/or the everlasting crown of glory (1 Pet. 5:4). Therefore, we should live always conscious of the following biblical verse:

> For we must all appear before the judgment seat of Christ; that every one may receive the things done in his body, according to that he hath done, whether it be good or bad.
>
> —2 Corinthians 5:10, kjv

Chapter 14

CONCLUSION

ONE OF THE saddest things in the body of Christ is the reality of false doctrine. So many pastors, prophets, apostles, teachers, and faithful church members embrace it because they are not familiar enough with the Word of God to realize it is unfaithful to the truth. Everything that is preached, all concepts we hear spoken in the name of Jesus, we must compare to what is written in the New Testament to test their veracity. Many things are supported with Bible verses, but we must always be ready to ask ourselves if the passages used are being manipulated and twisted to mean something other than the truth. This can sometimes make it necessary to look at the original Greek or Hebrew. Also, the context must always be considered, and we must seek God's revelation through the marvelous Holy Spirit, who is here on Earth to help us with such matters.

All who truly desire to follow the one true God should dedicate themselves to prayer and Bible study to discover the real truth of His Word. As God then uncovers the core of His will for us, we are confronted with a choice, a life-changing decision to make. We need to decide where the seeds of God's Word will fall in our life (Luke 8:4–15). Will they fall on the rocky soil, where we receive God's message with joy but lack deep roots and after a while fall away when facing temptation? Or will they fall among the thorns, so that, after following Jesus for a while, His message gradually drains away from our life because the cares and worries and riches of this life are more important to us? Or will they fall on good soil? Will we cling on to God's message of hope and through a life of obedience, dedicated to Him, without straying to the right or to the left? If we do this, we will produce a plentiful harvest, with eternal life as the result.

This is a decision every person who knows God's good news about Jesus Christ must make. We need to determine whether we will give up everything to follow Him or not. There is no halfway house. We cannot give up just a bit of our lives, more or less abiding by Jesus, and keep the rest. If we do that, we will live life deceiving ourselves, thinking we will go to heaven, but in fact we will not. We need to count the cost (Luke 14:28–34) and come to a conclusion of either 100 percent commitment to Him or 0 percent.

In Revelation, after the seven messages are given to each of the seven churches, there is a call to remain faithful (Rev. 2:11, 17, 26–28). Even if we are God's elect and are even honored by God, as Jeroboam son of Nephat, king of Israel, and Josiah, king of Judah, were, it is still possible to fall. Not even wisdom can keep us from falling. It didn't for Solomon. We must rely on God's grace, perseverance, and a fearful heart before God, totally dedicated to seeking Him. If you are only 40 percent committed to God, or even 80 percent or 98 percent or 99 percent, you need to stop and commit 100 percent of yourself to Him in every area and part of your life and start living a holy life.

Our choice is therefore either to be a slave to sin, which leads to "everlasting destruction" (2 Thess. 1:9, KJV), or to wholly obey God, which leads to righteous living and everlasting life (Acts 6:22–23).

Those who believe in their hearts they are made right with God and confess they are saved (Rom. 10:10) have made the right decision to follow Christ and are saved by faith alone. Once saved, as part of our covenant with Jesus Christ, we must do everything humanly possible to please the Lord and obey His teachings in order to remain so. It's not easy to get into heaven (Matt. 7:14), and if we're not submissive to God, we won't be allowed access. We can never act the same way as the world because we are citizens of heaven, so our inheritance is incorruptible.

Christ has accomplished all that was necessary for us to have a right relationship with God and therefore receive eternal life, but "merely listening to the law doesn't make us right with God. It is obeying the law that makes us right in his sight" (Rom. 2:13, NLT). James explains this concept further by emphasizing that our faith is only alive and of worth when our works prove it (James 2:14). Becoming a Christian is one thing, and acting like Jesus is another. We do not earn our salvation by works, but our works carried out through love prove the salvation within. Salvation is accomplished internally, and it requires effort and sacrifice on our part to do this. It is a gift from God that needs to be nurtured and matured in order to come to full fruition (1 Pet. 2:2–3), for example, we need to be actively helping the poor in order to be saved (Matt. 25:34–46).

Of course, if the saved person dies as soon as they make the decision to obey Christ, then this is not relevant. However, for us who are still on the earth after the initial decision of complete obedience to Jesus, every day we live, we run the risk of losing eternal life if we do not stay close to God and to His ways. The Lord calls our faith into action and attitudes.

> Do to others whatever you would like them to do to you. This is the essence of all that is taught in the law and the prophets.
> —MATTHEW 7:12, NLT

A result of living by faith according to God's high standard of holiness means we will be free from the power of sin, as slaves of God. We are also given the gift of fullness of life (John 10:10), complete joy (John 15:11), and the abundant comfort of the Holy Spirit, as well as the gifts of righteousness and peace.

The Holy Spirit is our help and our strength to guide us in the right way of living (John 16:8–11) and in turning away from sin, so all our decisions are to be made under His supervision. He dwells within us (Rom. 8:9), making us aware of God's truth, and acts as a sanctifying deposit of our salvation (Eph. 1:13), revealing our sonship (Gal. 4:6).

We are to be "controlled" and "led" by Him (Rom. 8:9, NIV; 8:14), enabling us to live a holy life in obedience to God's Word. This does not guarantee perfection for us because we are still fallible and prone to mistakes and sinning and are even limited by our own understanding and carnal desires. But our hope is in God. He is always faithful to forgive, although we need to be wary of repeatedly and purposefully sinning after becoming born again, because without true repentance and turning away from the old ways, we will be treated as enemies of God (Heb. 10:26–31).

Bible study is a rock and will keep us from falling. God's Word has the power to cure our souls, to guide our feet (Prov. 6:23), to comfort us (Ps. 119:52), and build us up (Acts 20:32). His words are peace-giving (Ps. 119:165) and sweeter than honey (Ps. 119:103). They are to be worn on the hands and forehead (Deut. 6:8–9), meaning they should remain at the forefront of our minds and always guide our actions. We should desire His Word more than gold (Ps. 19:10), and like fire in the heart, it purifies us (Eph. 5:26). Without it, we will die spiritually (Matt. 4:4), and it is necessary in order for us to grow in wisdom and understanding (Luke 8:18).

There are consequences of not learning or feeding off God's Word for the Christian. For example, Uzzah, who died immediately after touching the ark to steady it in 1 Chronicles 13:9, had good intentions. However, he lacked knowledge of and reverence for God's law, so he disobeyed it. The consequence was death. There was a commandment behind manhandling the ark, and God had to honor His word. Through this, God has revealed the power and truth behind His Word to us and the importance of reading, studying, and learning it.

What keeps us from falling and what helps us remain close to the Father's heart is His grace. God's grace empowers us to turn from what is unrighteous and live a holy life. Without His divine help, it would be impossible to live according to His law. Grace is also an essential factor for spiritual growth. When we submit every part of our lives to Him, He is faithful to pour it out on us. And remember that God is impartial. If there is anyone who enjoys His grace, anointing, and authority more than you, it's probably because that person is desiring and seeking Him more than you. Whoever seeks God, he or she will receive (Matt. 7:8).

We need to be alert to the temptation of even thinking we can do anything in our own strength, because then we will forfeit God's power, strength, and ability to help us obey Him and live up to His standards. This would make us truly deceived and proud. Never forget that when we do fail to obey and relinquish His grace, if we repent with sincere hearts, we will be forgiven and can continue on our Christian walk.

We need to really recognize we have fallen short and acknowledge we cannot do anything—absolutely anything—without His help. We can't fulfill any commandment or live any sort of holy life at all on our own because we're too weak and feeble. When we are utterly convinced of this in the depth of our soul, we will understand through and through that in our weakness He is strong, so the only way to live up to His high standard of holiness is through Him working in us, through our relationship with Him. We are nothing. He is our everything. We do not lack a thing in this life (Ps. 23:1) because God is all we need, and He's our Pastor. This does not mean that He never lets us go without food, drink, money, or clothes, but because we arrive at the point where His presence and love satisfies us so much, we don't even feel such a great need for these material provisions. We get less and less as the Lord gets greater and greater in us.

In this way, we will wholly let go of our own life, and therefore the only decisions we make are based on His leading, never our own desires. We will completely deny ourselves and give up all of our own wants and dreams, because our only disposition is for Him to direct us. Therefore, instead of praying, "Lord, let my dreams come true," we pray, "Lord, let Your dreams be realized in my life." Our aim is to arrive at a place where any time we have a desire or aspiration inside us, it hopefully could only ever be from Him. Nonetheless, we will then pray about these wills within us and give them over to Him in case they are not actually His. Just because our hearts desire something does not mean it is His will. God is more than capable of giving us something to do that we don't want to accomplish. We must be aware of the teaching to "just follow our heart," because sometimes our hearts may be wrong. Instead, we should be submissive and 100 percent subject to His desires and plans for us. Whoever doesn't do His will, will not be saved (1 John 2:17).

Unconditional love, obedience, and faithfulness toward God are crucial for our relationship with Him to be real. Our relationship with Him needs to be alive and active, manifest in constant personal purity, fruitfulness, and humility. Life is a relentless battle between good and evil, waging war against the flesh and the desire to rule our own life, which is only won by those who have found the meaning of life in Him. When we have our identity so caught up in His, then we know we have truly found the purpose for living.

When we live 100 percent for Him in all we are; when we put living for Him as the most important thing to be done on our daily agenda; when even dying for Him, suffering the greatest pain—whether emotional or physical—still does not separate us from His love and our faith in Him does not falter; when we put obedience to Him before everything, mockery and punishment from man; when we deny our own desires and what we think is best; when we reject our own logical reasoning because we have heard His call and fully understand the importance of obedience to God despite everything and everyone else going against it; when He is our first and foremost thought and desire every day; when prayer to Him and spending time in His presence is our first thought as we wake up to a new day; when His hand on our lives, hearing His voice, and fulfilling His will are our greatest wishes and we actively seek these things before anything else in our lives; when even if the worst thing ever happened in our lives, something that would make many question, Where was God? we do not fall and abandon the hope we have; if that still does not make us doubt God's power and existence, and we still love and trust Him the same; when we come to the understanding that God is the essence of our lives—all that we have and are, all the good that we see comes from His glorious thoughts and creativity—and we thank Him for everything, whether good or bad, then, only then, can we really believe we are striving to live to please Him, in His strength.

The meaning of life is, after initially receiving salvation from Jesus Christ, remaining firm in our relationship with God.

TO CONTACT THE AUTHOR

info@wordsarenotenoughministry.org
www.wordsarenotenoughministry.org